The Development Crisis

THE DEVELOPMENT CRISIS

Blueprint for Change

by
Carlos Geraldo Langoni
Foreword by Paul A. Volcker

International Center
for Economic Growth

Affiliated with the
Institute for Contemporary Studies

TO MY FAMILY   VERA

BERNARDO

EDUARDO

PATRICIA

Inquiries, book orders, and catalog requests should be addressed to International Center for Economic Growth, 243 Kearny Street, San Francisco, CA 94108 (415) 981-5353.

Book design and production by Marian Hartsough

Library of Congress Cataloging-in-Publication Data

Langoni, Carlos Geraldo.
    The development crisis.

    Translation of: Crise do desenvolvimento.
    Bibliography: p. 147.
    Includes index.
    1. Monetary policy—Brazil. 2. Debts, External—
Brazil. 3. Debt relief—Brazil. 4. Monetary Policy—
Developing Countries. 5. Debts, external—Developing
countries. 6. Debt relief—Developing countries.
7. International Monetary Fund. I. Title.

HG835.L3613 1987   336.3'0981   87-29350
ISBN 0-917616-95-2
ISBN 0-917616-94-4 (pbk.)

Table of Contents

Table and Figures

Preface

Difficulties in finding solutions to the LDC debt crisis are aggravated by conflicting perceptions of what the essence of the crisis is. The developed countries see the problem as a debt crisis, while the LDCs themselves see it as a crisis in development. *The Development Crisis: Blueprint for Change* reflects this important LDC viewpoint.

In publishing this book, the International Center for Economic Growth makes available to the English-speaking policy audiences an important new perspective on the present quandary. Carlos Geraldo Langoni's outlook is that of a former LDC central bank president who led his country's debt rescheduling negotiations and managed its monetary policy through a year of the crisis. The book was originally published in Portuguese for an audience in the author's native Brazil. It has been expanded and updated to reflect recent events and to address the interests of a worldwide audience.

Although Mr. Langoni centers his attention on the Brazilian experience, he shows the extent to which the debt crisis is part of a major, worldwide economic adjustment. This adjustment has involved and affected all nations, as well as the international public and private financial institutions. The major burden, however, has fallen on the LDCs. Langoni argues that restoring economic growth and human development will require adjustments by the LDCs *and* complementary, consistent, and coherent actions by the developed countries and the international financial institutions.

ICEG offers this book as a contribution to strengthening the partnership among countries and institutions that understand the importance of economic growth as a means to improve the lives of individuals and the balance of wealth among nations.

> Nicolas Ardito-Barletta
> General Director
> International Center for Economic Growth

Panama City, Panama
September, 1987

Foreword

Carlos Langoni has qualifications that, in combination, are uniquely suited to making intelligent analysis of the international debt crisis accessible to a large readership.

He is, to start with, a solidly-trained economist. He was head of the central bank of Brazil—Latin America's largest country and largest debtor—in 1982 when the crisis struck, and was engaged first-hand in the efforts to contain and diffuse it. His present position as Director of the Getulio Vargas Foundation, the leading Brazilian economic research center, has provided a vantage point for both reflection and analysis. He is, at the same time, an advisor and participant in financial markets, a practical man of affairs, aware of the opportunities as well as the pressures emerging from the debt crisis. He is, not least for present purposes, articulate in English!

Readers of *The Development Crisis: Blueprint for Change* are the beneficiaries of Mr. Langoni's talents and experience in all these respects. He places the debt crisis against the larger backdrop of the development strategy adopted by most of Latin America in the earlier postwar period—a strategy that, he emphasizes, was becoming exhausted by the 1980s. As Mr. Langoni sees it, the crisis has forced a rethinking of the older approach characterized by heavy governmental intervention in the economy, widespread subsidies and protectionism, all supported by large borrowings. He looks toward a new approach, toward growth consistent with greater economic and political freedom.

But if that promise is to be fulfilled, more than internal reform will be required. Ways and means will have to be found to deal constructively with external economic and financial restraints. Mr. Langoni offers specific suggestions to that end.

One need not agree with every one of his proposals and recommendations to recognize the relevance of the issues he raises; the technical sophistication with which he considers the detailed institutional, negotiating, and financial issues; and his understanding of the larger economic and political setting—within and without Latin America—in which these more technical questions need to be resolved.

To my [possibly prejudiced!] mind, Mr. Langoni's broad approach is consistent with the objectives and precepts of the "debt strategy" as adopted in 1982 and particularly as reinforced in 1985 by Secretary Baker at the IMF-World Bank meetings in Seoul. And I found it both interesting and encouraging that some of his specific points about the role of the IMF and World Bank and the potential of certain financial techniques (such as debt-equity swaps) are precursors of some themes emphasized at the Washington IMF-IBRD meetings a few weeks ago.

Perhaps Mr. Langoni would not agree with so positive an assessment of the present strategy, conscious as he is of the extent to which past efforts to deal with the debt crisis, however benign the objectives, have in implementation fallen short in important areas. Nor would I for one, agree with the wisdom or practicality of every suggestion in his new book. But I think thoughful readers will come away with a better sense of the nature and size of the challenge, of the enormous stakes in terms of Latin American growth and prosperity, and of the basic ingredients for a successful resolution.

Paul A. Volcker,
October 5, 1987

Introduction

The current Latin American debt crisis holds some urgent lessons for the world community. My viewpoint on this topic is that of an ex-official, a central banker in one Latin country who saw an economic golden age turn rather quickly into a nightmare, and who for several years struggled to meet each day's obligations and move on to the next. In 1983 I resigned my post as president of Brazil's Central Bank and began to devote most of my time to talking with others about the experience, and thinking and writing about it. These pages are intended to communicate a Latin's view of what happened, how, and why, and to offer some ideas toward a conceptual framework for national and international policies that can get us all through the crisis and onto a more orderly course of development.

From my point of view, a major theme has emerged from the welter of events and circumstances subject to retrospective analysis: we—Latin governments, American leaders, banks of other industrialized nations, multilateral economic institutions, and others—all contributed to the problem. It was not simply a question of Latins borrowing too much:

a borrower borrows from a lender, and third parties make the rules. Aggressive lending by international banks and the hesitancy of both the International Monetary Fund (IMF) and developing nation central banks to intervene when needed were but three of the outside forces that stimulated — or at least failed to moderate — the Latin acquisition of excessive debt. It is my hope that as the reader travels with me through the experiences of recent years and shares in my analysis of the events and issues, he or she will agree that both moral responsibility and practical reality call not for demands from others that Latin Americans get their house in order, but for a mutual process of planning and action; not for directives and finger-pointing, but for negotiation; not for displays of relative economic or political power, but for mutual respect in seeking solutions that will put us on a path to orderly economic growth.

The immediate concern of the economic community in 1982 was, of course, to reschedule the foreign debts that could no longer be serviced. In order to escape this external liquidity trap and reach a new stage of self-sustained growth, a three-dimensional adjustment process is needed — among the developing countries, within the international finance system (including both banks and multilateral institutions), and among the major industrialized economies. After five years of rescheduling, most debtor countries are still excessively vulnerable to external events; they are on a path of irregular economic performance, suggesting that the global adjustment process has fallen well below everyone's initial expectations.

Participants in the debt negotiations continue to pursue conventional refinancing schemes. New levels of credit are being set primarily to reduce bank exposure rather than to attend to the minimum financial needs of developing countries. Key issues such as interest rate levels and the creation of devices to protect against external shocks have been kept off the table.

Adjustments within the debtor countries also have been quite limited. Steady growth cannot be reached until Latin American inflation is stabilized. Control of inflation requires both changing the external conditions that aggravate it and implementing wide-ranging domestic policies to bring it under control. Recent Brazilian experience shows that even a comprehensive indexation program cannot prevent the damage caused by inflation. Quite the opposite: indexing becomes an added constraint on the economy, increasing its vulnerability to external shocks and accelerating the momentum of domestic price increases. It is crucial to alter inflationary expectations themselves, which means much more than bringing greater skill to the management of aggregate demand. It calls for redefinition of the relationship between the state and society, between the government and private economic institutions.

What we are now witnessing in Latin America is the exhaustion of a development strategy based on government expansion funded through domestic and foreign borrowing. Granting subsidies to the private sector in order to assuage its unhappiness at the competitive expansion of government has proved a self-defeating strategy: it just aggravates the debt. Instead, limits need to be imposed on the intervention, direct or indirect, of the state in the economy. Just as there is a need for mutuality in the economic community, within each developing country relationships must be redefined. The state needs to resume the role of agent for change on behalf of the public, rather than acting as an endogenous contributor to internal imbalances. Each nation has the challenge of designing and bringing about a new internal framework that will free the sources of economic growth, in particular by giving room to the private sector.

I firmly believe that long-term economic growth can occur only in an atmosphere of greater political and economic freedom than now exists in most less-developed countries (LDCs). In my country, we expect wide-ranging and deep institutional reforms in the next few years — politically, economically, and socially. It is a historic opportunity to lay the foundations for a new society in which more and more wealth is generated and its distribution is less unequal.

I will begin by tracing the origins of the present crisis back to the 1960s. In chapter 1, I draw on Brazil's experience over fifteen years to show how the strategy of growth with indebtedness was born, grew up, and suffered a sudden and premature death. Chapter 2 examines the experience since 1982, when the world learned, first from Poland, then from Mexico, that national default was real, and that massive debt restructuring would have to take place in Latin America, or major parts of the world economy would be in grave trouble. I believe that the material presented shows that the current rescheduling procedure is not a definitive solution to the debt problem, either for the international financial system or for the Latin countries. A tentative outline for a long-term alternative strategy is offered.

Next, the relationship between external and internal adjustment is examined, first through the conservative lens of the IMF (Chapter 3), then through the eyes of developing countries (Chapter 4). In Chapter 3, the uneven performance of the IMF is highlighted by citing some methodological inconsistencies in its traditional stabilization programs and showing how these have distorted and hindered attempts to reach a sound solution. A redefinition of IMF's role is proposed, with concrete lines of action. In Chapter 4, the focus is on domestic actions taken in response to the debt crisis. Based on analysis of this experience, I try to demonstrate that there are institutional changes and policy revisions that, if adopted by a country (providing that needed changes also occur in the behavior of outside parties, and that luck is good), could curb inflation and lead to long-term economic growth.

The last chapter offers an agenda for the future: a new development strategy based on extensive evaluation of the methods and concepts that have gotten us where we are. Recommendations are offered for changes both at the international and domestic levels. The basic challenge is how to manage our way out of the crisis and, at the same time, to enhance the prospects for sound and steady long-term growth. A resumption of economic growth cannot be taken for granted. The economic forces that could accomplish this crucial objective have been set awry by the tumble of events and decisions. Deliberate action is needed to remove both internal rigidities — usually the intrusion of the state into affairs best left private — and external restraints, particularly the brutal squeeze on the availability of long-term credit.

I have discussed the main topics of this book with my students at the Graduate School of Economics of the Getulio Vargas Foundation. Friends also have supported and stimulated my thinking at different stages. In particular, Armando Paulo Silva, Og Leme, Jorge de Souza, and Edy Kogut patiently read, discussed, and helped proofread earlier versions. Vicentte de Carvalho and Altino Augusto de Oliveira helped me with the basic statistics. Many others have also contributed indirectly through a generous word of encouragement or a kind gesture of friendship. Among the many, particular acknowledgments are due to Fernando Moreira, Carlos Balbino, Antonio de Oliveira Santos, Silvio Pedroza, Luis and Maurilio Biago, Antonio Salles, Bertoldo Probebinsky, Carlos Alberto Vieira, Jose Barbosa Mello, Walder Goes, Oscar Bloch, Guilherme Cartolano, Dalton and Augusto Lins, Osiris Ribeiro, and Mozart Theophilo. For the English version, special thanks to Rick White, economics editor at the Institute for Contemporary Studies. This book is also dedicated to them, with my gratitude.

Summary of Recommendations

Debt Negotiations

We should move away from conventional debt *refinancing* toward a new and more realistic stage of debt *restructuring*. This new debt adjustment program should result from a process of *negotiation among partners in the world financial system* — the debtor nation governments, lender nation governments, lending banks, and multilaterals. The program should be part of a *long-term plan* to restore the financial market for the debtor country, solve the problem of its external debt, and put the country on a path to economic growth.

The plan should include the following:

- A level of *long-term external resources* sufficient to reverse the outflow of capital and sustain development. Lenders must accept that LDCs need to be able to run a certain level of current account deficit to sustain growth.

- A flexible negotiated external interest rate with *automatic capitalization of differentials* observed between the market rate and a long-term shadow rate to be applied to rescheduling.

- *Debtor country performance goals with a long-term focus.* A time schedule should be negotiated that is appropriate for each country, with assessment based on overall performance rather than on adherence to every item and date in the implementation plan.

- Responsibility by the industrialized nations to *consider the effect on LDCs* when determining international trade policies, domestic interest rate policies, posture toward multilateral agencies, and other financial issues.

Performance Measures for LDCs

The measures to be used for LDCs in meeting adjustment goals should aim at evaluating the *quality* of performance. The program should be judged on the *consistency* of policies and their *implementation* with the adjustment goals rather than on short-term quantitative measurements.

Two *complementary indicators* are needed to obtain a consistent analysis of the evolution of public deficit: the nominal deficit, as it has been measured by the IMF, and the operational deficit. If both are growing, no progress is being made toward adjustment of the public sector. Growth in the nominal deficit alone is inconclusive.

To evaluate the structural makeup of the public deficit so that constructive corrective actions can be taken, *the operational deficit should be broken down into components* and each component examined.

Structural variables should be employed by the IMF side-by-side with its conventional short-term variables. Structural measurements would test the relationship between policy implementation and long-term performance. Private investment, import levels, and social indicators are examples of structural conditionalities that should undergo yearly review to make sure that policies are working.

The short-term automatic relationship between internal adjustment and access to negotiated funds should be eliminated. In this area, greater emphasis needs to be given to developing countries' *external* performance, within a longer time frame, e.g., at least a year.

The International Finance System

The financial market for the debtor countries needs to be restored. Profound, orderly, consistent action will be required to shock the financial system into a new set of expectations and behaviors. Such action must include a change in the policies of industrialized countries, innovation by the multilateral institutions, and particularly the IMF, new mechanisms to deal with short-term liquidity problems and long-term restructuring of debt, and a new agreement between debtors and lenders. Logical connections need to be established between short- and long-term policies, between temporary adaptation and structural changes, between adjustment and growth.

The voluntary withdrawal of private banks demands *more active participation by multilateral institutions* in financing the developing countries.

- The IMF needs to be given *increased political power and enhanced financial resources*. It needs to take on greater operational flexibility, so that countries can approach it voluntarily for help when they anticipate future difficulty.

- *More concert is needed between the IMF and the World Bank*; this should result from recognizing the infeasibility of distinguishing between adjustment and development in the prevailing world context.

- *The Club of Paris should be enlarged* by including representatives of advisory committees to the private banks. It then should deal not only with government debts but also with the basic guidelines for renegotiation between banks and countries. It might become an international forum for achieving consensus on long-term solutions to the problem of external indebtedness.

- The recent trend among major banks to increase loan-loss reserves reflects a positive step in the direction of sound, realistic solutions. It creates concrete opportunities for the implementation of new innovative schemes: different forms of interest capitalization and even a voluntary reduction in the debt stock through the *issuing of a new class of long-term bonds* with real collateral, rather than just IMF programs, would allow countries to internalize some of the current debt discounts quoted in the secondary market.

- The *debt equity swap* is a new and positive market development. Developing countries should take advantage of this opportunity as a useful hedge against the extraordinary level of uncertainty dampening private investment.

Internal Reform in Brazil

Just as a dramatic demonstration of change is needed in the world economic community to create a shock to economic expectations, wide and deep reforms are required internally. *Control of the state needs to be returned to society.* The role of the public sector in the economy needs to be greatly reduced. Redirection of the public deficit should no longer be seen as a budgetary matter but as the driving force behind institutional reorganization of the economy.

Control of inflation is a key objective in restoring self-sustained growth. Past experience has shown that generalized indexation loses its effectiveness by neutralizing the allocative and distributive distortions associated with rising inflation. The result is a fall in capital accumulation, leading to stagnation.

- *Congress should take over effective control of major spending decisions* now centralized in the executive branch.
- *There should be a unified budget* for the country and a simple monetary program whereby targets for growth of the key monetary aggregates are set to stabilize the overall price level.
- *Subsidies of all types should either be eliminated or appear explicitly in the public sector budget as current expenditures or investment, depending on their nature.* The public deficit should be permanently reduced and controlled.
- Basically what is needed is a *massive reallocation of resources* (a) from the oversized and inefficient public sector to the more dynamic private sector, and (b) from overprotected domestic activities toward export expansion and diversification.

- The *Central Bank should be given more freedom to act* without interference from either the executive or the legislative branches of government, by making it equidistant from these branches and giving it legal authority to stabilize overall price levels. Direct or indirect financing of public spending should be prohibited by law.

- *Compulsory indexation should be eliminated gradually* right after the announcement of these reforms and replaced by voluntary market mechanisms. Managed floating exchange rates should replace the crawling peg system. Wages should be set by free bargaining through direct negotiations rather than by the present system of automatic monthly correction. *Ex post facto* indexation should be retained only for long-term savings as insurance against inflation.

- It is fundamental to *keep domestic interest rates positive* in real terms and *further develop the internal capital market.*

- The state should *return to its role as a social agent*, as an instrument consolidating the economic infrastructure, and as a vehicle supporting the research necessary for innovation.

- Brazil should *strengthen its successful transition from import substitution to export expansion.* There is still a wide scope for reallocating resources toward tradeable goods through a coherent exchange rate policy.

- Finally, *greater emphasis needs to be given to the absorption of new risk capital*, reversing the current trend toward increasing discrimination against foreign investment.

1

The Roots of the Crisis

Until the mid-1960s, most economic growth in Brazil took place with very limited external borrowing. The main sources of credit were governments, especially export agencies. We also received development funds from multilateral organizations—chiefly the World Bank and the Inter-American Development Bank (IDB). Borrowing from commercial banks outside the country was limited to short-term commercial loans. Within this context there was no room for significant external account imbalances to mount. In fact, from 1960 to 1970, Brazilian current account deficits stayed at an average of one percent of gross domestic product (GDP).

When in 1964 Brazilian planning minister Roberto Campos traveled to foreign capitals such as Washington and London, his major concern was dealing with the governments about trade arrears. Such visits as he made to private banks were incidental. These banks were just beginning to think about the potential profits that might come from stepping up their international loans. Dollar deposits outside the United States were still minor—in their embryonic stage, as it later appeared.

The key feature of this early period was the fact that the supply of external credit was limited by domestic budget constraints and the foreign trade balances of the lender countries. Domestic investment plans of developing countries could not automatically be covered by external loans. Before 1967, the Brazilian economy enjoyed a period of growth without indebtedness — not as a result of deliberate strategy, but simply because sources of foreign credit were limited.

The Golden Age

In the late 1960s, the role played by private banks in the international financial market began a marked expansion. This new development was stimulated by the domestic imposition of restrictions upon financial markets — particularly interest rate controls, such as Regulation Q in the United States — and was fed by a growing U.S. current account deficit.

The OPEC oil price cartel of 1973 gave a giant boost to the banks' newly expanded role in international lending. Massive financial surpluses in oil-producing countries had to be recycled back to deficit countries, where the money was needed, among other reasons, to purchase more oil. The private money center banks were the natural channel, accepting oil-nation deposits and lending the dollars both locally and overseas.

Throughout the 1970s, the world money market was consolidated and organized on the basis of a complex and sophisticated interregional network prepared to operate — literally — twenty-four hours a day. Dollar deposits outside the United States, "Eurodollars," attracted a growing number of private investors. The international flow was fed by major regional money centers extending from Hong Kong to Panama, from London and New York to Bahrain and Singapore. The credit-generating potential of these centers is high, not only because of the low margin of compulsory reserves they require (when it exists at all), but also because of the leverage of interbank deposits. The interbank feeder subsystem speeds the intermediation mechanism, since smaller banks with limited branch facilities can take in deposits through larger banks.

The money market is then both extremely efficient and highly unstable.

The interbanking mechanism opens the door to new members and enhances market competitiveness. For each new link in the deposit chain, costs are added and passed on to another bank or to final borrowers. It is easy to see that, side by side with this chain of growing costs, a sequence of higher risks and lower liquidity develops. It should be stressed that profits can be made only within the spread between borrowing and lending rates.

The system is pro-cyclical: it endogenously accelerates any drive toward expansion, and symmetrically exacerbates any contractionist trend. Other factors compound instability. The essential feature of financial mediation is the effort to reconcile the interests of lenders and borrowers. Lenders strive to enhance liquidity by making short-term loans, while borrowers — particularly large corporations and countries — attempt to defer as far as possible the dates on funds borrowed. Because of the volume of funds involved and the relatively free market for Eurodollars, mediation between these two objectives becomes highly sophisticated, allowing deposits averaging six months to support loans more than ten years in maturity. The combination of low-liquidity assets and highly liquid liabilities is an additional complication at times of crisis. Furthermore, since these dollar operations are developed outside financial domestic systems, appropriate liquidity rediscount mechanisms are not always available to deal with problems.

Until 1978 the international financial market combined plenty of liquidity with relatively low interest rates: this explains its continuous expansion in the decade of the 1970s except for some episodic crises.

This well-oiled machine — capitalism at its most efficient — found the ideal loan clientele in developing countries, mainly those with a growing industrial sector. Even before the first oil shock, some of these countries tried to take advantage of the new international money market to tap new sources of funds. In 1967, Brazilian public and private corporations were given permission by the government to borrow abroad, either directly or through a transfer of funds borrowed by domestic banks.[1] The Central Bank set limits on minimum maturity and maximum cost. Thus the development-*cum*-indebtedness strategy was launched.

TABLE 1.1 Basic Indicators of the Brazilian Foreign Sector

| Years | Current Account Deficit | | External Debt | | | | International Reserves[b] (US$ million) |
	Balance (US$ million)	Percentage of GDP	Gross Debt[a] (US$ million)	Ratio of Interest Payments to Exports (%)	Ratio of Debt Service to Exports (%)		
1960	− 478	1.9	2,534	9	42		115
1970	− 562	1.3	5,295	9	54		1,187
1980	− 12,396	4.9	53,848	31	65		6,913
Selected periods							
1967	− 237	0.7	3,332	11	38		199
1973	− 1,688	2.1	12,572	8	42		6,416
1974	− 7,122	6.8	17,166	8	33		6,269
1978	− 6,015	2.3	43,511	21	64		11,895
1979	− 10,021	4.3	49,904	27	70		9,689
1982	− 14,755	5.2	70,198	56	97		3,994
1983	− 6,171	3.0	81,319	44	90		4,563
1984	+ 517	0	91,091	38	67		11,995
1985	+ 302	0	95,857	38	77		7,690
1986	− 4,849	1.1	101,540	41	99		4,585

Source: Central Bank of Brazil

[a] Registered, medium and long term
[b] International liquidity, IMF concept

Brazil's foreign debt grew from US$3.3 billion in 1967 to US$12.6 billion in 1973. Private banks were increasingly the source of foreign loans. The growing inflow of external savings helped speed economic growth, which reached record levels in the period 1970–1973. The current account deficit grew, but remained at a moderate level: around 2 percent of GDP in late 1973. The strategy looked like it had a good chance to succeed, chiefly because it was supported by a rapid expansion of exports.

The period 1967–1973 had two additional, significant characteristics. The trade balance fluctuated between mild surpluses and deficits, showing no trend toward disequilibrium. The foreign debt was therefore caused not by a need to finance imbalances, but rather by a desire to attract foreign capital. On the other hand, access to the financial market was so easy that it became common to borrow abroad merely to accumulate foreign currency reserves. This reserve, as collateral, in turn made it easier for more loans to be obtained from international banks: the criterion employed by banks in their country-risk analyses was the relationship of a nation's export growth to its interest rates at that time highly favorable for Brazil. In fact, the ratio of interest to export revenue was reduced from 11 percent to 8 percent during that period. If we include amortizations, i.e., if we work with the debt service/exports ratio, we find that this indicator grew only slightly until 1975 (Table 1.1).

International banks, for their part, were fascinated; they had found the philosopher's stone at last. These new customers, the newly industrialized countries, apparently combined the uncombinable: high yield and low risks. The term sovereign risk, used to qualify loans to countries, was elegant enough to justify the rapid expansion of private credit. Banks began to prepare themselves to deal with countries instead of just corporations. Special departments were set up and economists began work on studies of the future development of those countries' economies. The process was so dynamic and competition so intense that steps were often reversed: economic studies were used to justify loans already extended rather than to evaluate them in advance. International operations became the banks' main source of profits. Everything seemed conducive to a happy and lasting relationship. Some surprises were in store, however. The events of the 1970s laid the groundwork for the drama of 1982.

TABLE 1.2   **World Economic Indicators*** *(percent)*

Years	Real Rate of Growth (GDP)	Rate of Inflation	Commodities Prices (rate of variation)	Quantum of International Trade (rate of variation)
1970	2.4	6.0	3.6	9.0
1971	3.4	5.4	− 4.8	6.0
1972	5.7	4.7	13.3	9.0
1973	6.3	7.8	53.3	12.5
1974	0.3	13.4	27.9	5.0
1975	− 1.2	11.3	− 16.2	− 4.0
1976	5.2	8.6	17.2	11.0
1977	3.7	8.9	21.2	5.0
1978	3.9	8.0	5.1	5.5
1979	3.3	9.8	23.7	6.5
1980	1.2	12.9	15.9	1.5
1981	1.2	10.6	− 11.3	1.5
1982	− 0.3	8.0	− 17.0	4.5
1983	2.3	5.5	− 10.6	− 3.3
1984	4.7	5.0	26.6	8.8
1985	3.0	4.5	− 10.3	3.7
1986	2.5	2.75	4.8	3.7

Source: IMF
*OECD country members

The First Adjustment Challenge

Universal growth, low inflation rates, and trade expansion: an idyllic setting in retrospect. Now it seems like a mirage. But such was life until 1973, when OPEC dropped its bomb, freeing inflationary tensions and creating its own dimension of disequilibrium.

The years 1970 and 1971 already had seen the weakening of the fixed exchange rate system established at the Bretton Woods Conference.[2] Exchange flexibility was essential for countries to regain control over their domestic policies. The quick growth of international reserves in Europe — fed by current account deficits in the United

States — had stimulated monetary expansion, which in turn intensified inflationary pressures that sooner or later would have to be dealt with. The fourfold rise in oil prices in 1973 was the perfect ingredient to convert potential inflation into actual inflation. By the late 1970s inflation rates in developed countries would double, on average, to a level of 10 percent, while growth would turn cyclical, alternating between recession and modest recovery (Table 1.2). There was nothing left of the strong, steady growth and low inflation of the postwar years.

Nearly all oil-importing countries — both developed and developing — had to decide how to address the severe disequilibrium in their foreign accounts produced by the oil shock. At this point, paths diverged: the developed countries chose to adjust promptly, and as a result quickly reduced their current account deficits, though at the cost of slower growth. In contrast, most developing countries decided to finance the external disequilibrium by using intensively their new access to the international financial market.

In fact, the two approaches are closely connected: access to international banks by developing countries expanded because developed countries were not competing with them for the same financial sources. From 1974 to 1978, the average real interest rate was minus 1 percent In other words, literally subsidized funds were being lent at a cost below inflation — an offer no one could refuse. The developing countries thought they too had found the philosopher's stone.

It is interesting to note that in Brazil's case the imbalance in the 1974 external account was higher than that in 1982. The current account deficit as a percentage of GDP reached 6.8 percent that year, compared to 5.2 percent in 1982. The 1974 upheaval in the balance of payments was also more violent and sudden. In barely one year the current account deficit quadrupled to US$7.1 billion, while the trade balance went from a historically even position to one of substantial deficit. By contrast, the crisis in 1982 occurred with the trade balance in surplus. There were other important differences: in 1974, the source of disequilibrium was the trade account, primarily oil imports (Figure 1.1). In 1982, the main impact was felt in the capital account, with the sudden reversal of loan flows.

The qualitative differences between the two periods are much more significant than the quantitative ones. The key difference was the exis-

FIGURE 1.1   Changes in Petroleum Prices

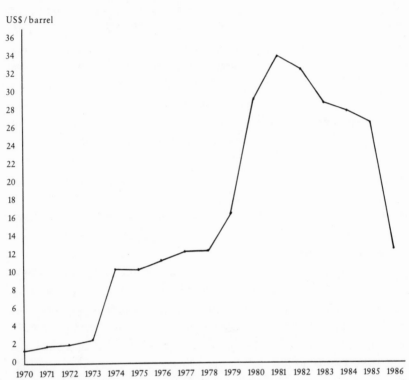

US$/barrel

Source: Central Bank

tence of a financial market. In 1974, it was possible to finance imbalances. In 1982, as we will see later, this possibility no longer existed.
The source of the crisis can be traced directly to the virtual closing of
the financial market.

Unlike the preceding period, after 1974 external financing was
no longer a mechanism solely for attracting foreign savings; it became
instrumental in coping with imbalances. Each year it was necessary
to obtain external funds to cover the expected current account deficit.
Brazil increasingly looked to international financial markets for new
loans. The growth-with-indebtedness process went into a new stage

in which current account disequilibrium was aggravated by a growing outflow of service payments. External interest rate began to stand out as a key element in the performance of the balance of payments.

A gradualist approach to external imbalances adopted in 1974 helped to sustain economic growth, although at a more moderate pace. Its inevitable counterpart was a rapid increase in external borrowing. There were clear signs: imports stabilized at a new and higher level, making exports essential to achieving a trade balance; the exchange policy remained unchanged; public investments were stepped up to offset the slowdown of private investments prompted by a higher degree of uncertainty; a broad import-substitution program was set in motion; and finally, the inflation rate settled at a new level, suggesting a relatively neutral monetary policy.

The assumption that the oil shock was a temporary problem was implicit in the policy of financing the disequilibrium. A view then shared widely was that the new oil prices would not hold up too long. This explains the initial hesitation to invest in domestic oil and alcohol production. In the absence of new external disruptions, exports were expected to eliminate the trade deficit gradually and eventually to provide surpluses that would automatically resolve the increasing indebtedness.

Before 1978, this optimism received some support from the facts, despite the difficulty of keeping export growth at the brisk rate required by new debt rollover needs. The trade balance was back in equilibrium in 1977, but the critical ratio between debt servicing (amortization plus interest) and exports, though moderately on the rise in the early stage of development with indebtedness, began to grow substantially: from 33 percent in 1974 to 64 percent in 1978. These were the first signs of harsher constraints to come.

The Explosion Of Real Interest Rates

Expectations of a quick end to these conditions vanished with a new outbreak of OPEC actions and substantial changes in American anti-inflationary policies. The power of the oil cartel exceeded initial estimates. OPEC countries took advantage of the leeway provided by a

TABLE 1.3   Interest Rates and the Price of Oil

Years	Interest Rates (%)		Price of Oil (US$/barrel)
	Nominal[a]	Real[b]	
1970	8.76	2.76	1.48
1971	6.95	1.55	1.80
1972	5.97	1.17	2.05
1973	9.34	1.84	2.54
1974	11.17	− 0.33	10.53
1975	7.78	− 3.32	10.53
1976	6.24	− 1.36	11.27
1977	6.43	− 1.17	12.11
1978	9.16	+ 1.66	12.33
1979	12.15	4.15	16.83
1980	13.99	4.89	29.47
1981	16.62	7.38	34.43
1982	13.58	5.66	33.00
1983	9.89	4.16	29.40
1984	11.21	7.04	28.60
1985	8.65	3.48	27.20
1986	6.82	3.96	12.70

Source: Central Bank of Brazil
[a] Six month average LIBOR, yearly rates
[b] Deflated by the GDP deflator of industralized countries

slight recovery in the world economy after 1976 and the slow emergence of alternative energy sources (including petroleum production in non-OPEC countries) to force through a new oil price boost. The price escalation went much further than a mere correction for inflation (Table 1.3).

At the same time, the U.S. Federal Reserve decided to tighten money as a weapon against inflation, which was now threatening industrialized countries. American fiscal policy was still strongly expansionist, however, owing mostly to the rigidity of military and social spending. The combination of monetary stringency and fiscal expansion inevitably led to skyrocketing interest rates, which went from negative levels in real terms to high positive ones. In the late 1970s they reached unprecedented peaks of about 7 to 8 percent in real terms.[3]

Superimposed on the financial shock of a new oil price hike, these developments were a warning to those who had adopted the sustained development with indebtedness strategy. The impact was now felt on the trade account and on the debt service account simultaneously. It was no longer a matter of borrowing just to pay the oil bill, as in 1974, but also of borrowing to cover increased interest payments.

The spiral of world inflation following 1973 had largely ended the fixed interest rates available in previous times of price stability. Floating-rate loans were the only way to reconcile short-term borrowing and long-term lending in an inflationary period fraught with uncertainty. These loans had been introduced during the days of easy liquidity. Floating rates were low then, and hence particularly attractive.

The inevitable predominance of dollar-denominated loans made external interest rates heavily dependent on U.S. domestic policy. Thus, in addition to the risk in external interest rates that stems from inflationary expectations, a strictly institutional component was added, which by definition is hard to predict: the fluctuation of American monetary policy. The foundation was laid for the transition to crisis. At the end of the 1970s some governments still considered these conditions temporary; they expected the dynamism of exports gradually to restore equilibrium. The devaluation of the cruzeiro in 1979 was a clear indication of the deteriorating external situation; it was an attempt to restore the balance of Brazilian trade accounts (Figure 1.2).

Developments would show that efforts to boost exports would not alone be enough to solve the problem. The inherited debt (nearly $50 billion by late 1979) combined with rising external interest rates introduced an element of rigidity to the rollover of positions in the international financial market. Brazil's 1979 current account deficit grew significantly, to 4.3 percent of GDP, though it remained below 1974 levels. This time the task of financing it would be much harder.

Despite its problems, the international financial market was still working, and developing countries could still rely on it. Governments as well as private institutions believed that interest rates could not remain for long above their long-term equilibrium level, i.e., above the level of marginal productivity of capital. Yet, external liquidity conditions

FIGURE 1.2   **External Interest Rates**

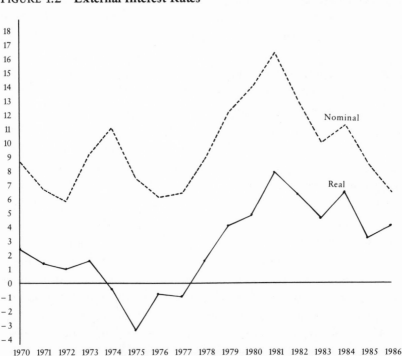

Source: Central Bank

were still favorable enough to justify the postponement of a drastic adjustment.

In fact, except for the exchange adjustment mentioned above, there was no clear sign of a *voluntary* adjustment strategy in Brazil before 1981. Fiscal and wage policies were openly expansionist and nearly all restrictive efforts were directed to the monetary sector. Sustained economic growth was thus achieved—7.2 percent in 1980—while inflation rates reached three digits (Table 1.4). External financing was becoming less workable however: debt servicing absorbed increasing shares of export revenue and jumped, between 1979 and 1982, from 70 per cent to 97 percent. With the combination of worldwide recession and high interest rates, exports were badly hit, and in 1982 they

TABLE 1.4   **Brazil: Inflation and Growth** *(percent)*

Years	Rate of Inflation[a]	Rate of growth of real GDP	
		Total	Per-capita
1970	19.3	8.3	6.2
1971	19.5	11.3	8.6
1972	15.7	12.1	9.3
1973	15.5	14.0	11.2
1974	34.5	9.0	6.4
1975	29.5	5.4	2.7
1976	46.3	10.1	7.4
1977	38.8	4.5	2.0
1978	40.8	4.7	2.2
1979	77.2	7.2	4.6
1980	110.2	9.1	6.5
1981	95.2	− 3.4	− 5.7
1982	99.7	0.9	− 1.5
1983	211.0	− 2.5	− 4.9
1984	220.6	5.7	3.1
1985	235.1	8.3	5.6
1986	65.0	8.2	5.5

Source: Getulio Vargas Foundation (GVF)

[a] General Price Index

suffered an absolute reduction for the first time in many years. The terms of trade (the ratio of export to import prices) showed negative performance — a drop of about 31 percent — owing to oil price increases and a sharp fall in the prices of major commodities.

Declining exports and interest rate increases therefore constituted a reversal in the performance of critical variables that had at first suggested that development with indebtedness would work. Still, the policy's sudden exhaustion came as something of a surprise: just when the voluntary adjustment was being implemented in 1981, with the resulting accumulation of trade balance surpluses, the Polish default, the Argentinian-British conflict, then the Mexican crisis shook the finan-

TABLE 1.5   Selected Items in Brazil's Balance of Payment (US$ million)

Years	Exports	Imports	Trade Balance	Oil Imports	Interest Payments (net)	Amortization	Currency Loans
1960	1,270	1,293	– 23	85	115	417	348
1970	2,739	2,507	+ 323	174	234	1,242	1,433
1980	20,132	22,955	– 2,823	9,368	6,311	6,689	10,596
Selected periods							
1967	1,654	1,441	+ 213	111	184	444	530
1973	6,199	6,192	+ 7	606	514	2,063	4,495
1974	7,951	12,641	– 4,690	2,558	652	1,943	6,642
1978	12,659	13,683	– 1,024	4,064	2,696	5,426	13,811
1979	15,244	18,084	– 2,840	6,263	4,186	6,527	11,228
1982	20,175	19,395	+ 780	9,566	11,353	8,098	13,419
1983	21,899	15,429	+ 6,470	7,470	9,555	10,061	8,152
1984	27,005	13,916	+ 13,089	6,867	10,203	7,816	7,612
1985	25,639	13,153	+ 12,486	5,694	9,659	10,160	4,871
1986[a]	22,393	12,866	+ 9,527	3,006	9,093	13,176	7,482

Source: Central Bank of Brazil
[a] Preliminary data

cial market, slamming the loan window shut on a large number of countries.

A question not yet addressed is whether the strategy could have worked in the absence of an oil shock. The answer must be strongly qualified: had the oil shock and spiraling interest rates not taken place, a number of the countries that tried to diversify their exports might have managed over time to progress successfully through the different stages of development with indebtedness (i.e., go smoothly through a maturation process from net importer of financial and real resources to net capital exporter). The key to a successful strategy would be to reverse the continuing growth of the debt service/export ratio, that would have entailed deliberately and realistically limiting indebtedness. On the other hand, even in the absence of external shocks, it would have been impossible for the economy to get healthy while continuing to incur indebtedness through excessive domestic spending.

In Latin America, the general trend toward indebtedness was brought about by a combination of elements: external credit went from being a genuine instrument for attracting investment funds to being a tool for financial rollovers, and later a way to cover higher oil bills and interest rate payments.[4] In such circumstances, a major change of direction had to be made. From the standpoint of cost, the ideal strategy was a process of adjustment based on market forces. This was attempted in 1981.[5]

Another important issue is why the financial market did not anticipate events. Governments operate under political constraints, and it is not surprising that they resist making unpopular adjustments. But banks are private institutions regulated by market forces. Why did the market not send out the right warnings to allow a gradual change in the flow of loans to developing countries?

Paradoxically, the market failed precisely because it is highly competitive: the differential between external and internal rates of return on banking operations was so high that banks were willing to run ever greater risks. Moreover, the mistaken view prevailed that country loans were risk-free. Banks fed on the illusion that their credits were allocated to specific self-financing projects rather than to balance-of-payments deficits (Table 1.5). Finally, access to basic information was poor for both individual countries and the overall financial system.

Lessons From the Mexican Default:
The Crisis Of 1982

With the Mexican default, banks suddenly discovered that they were as vulnerable as the developing nations. For some institutions, assets held in a handful of developing countries were three or four times greater than their own capital. A halt in interest payments might easily turn a highly profitable situation into a loss. In 1982/83 capital losses created by the necessity of recording only a small proportion of their loan assets as nonperforming credit would have been enough to send some of these banks into bankruptcy.

This situation partially explains the financial hysteria following the Mexican earthquake in 1982. Attempts by individual banks to correct several years' worth of overexposure in just a few months were held off only by the need to preserve the financial system as a whole. In the meantime, however, the drastic external liquidity crunch exerted strong recessionary pressures on a large number of developing countries.

Once triggered, the financial crisis was brutal in its impact and unexpected in its timing. Neither central banks nor commercial banks—let alone the governments of developing countries—were prepared to take the action that might at least have lessened its disruptive consequences. After the Mexican default it became clear that there was no worldwide institutional framework for dealing with the crisis in an orderly fashion.

On the contrary, the first reactions were clearly pro-cyclical and aggravated the situation. The best illustration of this was the August 1982 IMF meeting in Toronto. In the eye of the storm, the developed countries agreed that there was no need to take special measures, either to reinforce the capital of multilateral institutions or to establish a liquidity window to help those countries that were not yet directly involved. At that stage in the game, the industrialized countries seriously underestimated how far the shock waves would travel. They stressed their concern about the need for greater adjustment by developing countries, and sat back to wait for a natural market correction, presumably to be facilitated by lower interest rates and the expected recovery of the world economy.

Since 1982, more than thirty countries have gone through a painful and troublesome process of rescheduling[6] — a direct consequence of the virtual paralysis of markets brought on as commercial banks acted to protect themselves. Each bout of rescheduling added to the initial uncertainty.

The major central banks and the governments of industrialized countries bear an important responsibility for the disorderly way the crisis evolved. They continued to take a noninterventionist posture while the market was forcing a complete halt in loans to developing countries. The concept of country risk usually applied by commercial banks quickly turned into regional risk, covering whole continents — a blunt attempt to correct in a few months the overlending of many years. Central banks knew that individual moves by each bank quickly to reduce its own overexposure would eventually be frustrated by the destabilizing effects of these actions on the market as a whole. Such a process cannot be brought to an end spontaneously. It requires either action by the debtors, which means market disruption, or some compulsory action by the central banks and their governments, which means absorbing some of the problem or, in economic jargon, internalizing externalities.

In the first six months of 1982, Brazil was able to borrow normally in the market, at an average rate of $1.5 billion a month. Just after the Mexican default, Brazil's access to the market was cut in half. Automatic borrowing virtually disappeared in the last quarter of the year. Market borrowing was replaced by negotiated borrowing, and market forces by bureaucratic meetings.

At the time, there seemed to us Brazilians no reason for the radical overnight change in the bankers' view of Brazilian risk. Later, however, our experience showed that the credit market's tendency to shrink could not be altered by the adjustment policies of the developing countries, or even by the announcement of an agreement with the IMF. Brazil took two steps: in October 1982 it announced a series of measures designed to cut its current account deficit in half; in December it reached an agreement with the IMF. Negative market forces proved to be more powerful, however. The country lost about $4 billion in interbank deposits and $2 billion to 3 billion of trade-related lines of credit. The external liquidity squeeze tightened.

Nonintervention dogma is not applicable where there is no market. There has to be outside action to stop the drain of resources. The velocity and intensity of such liquidity leakages cannot be affected by any conceivable adjustment within the debtor countries.

Given the violent change in expectations and in the approach to risk, an early agreement with the IMF would not have been enough to reverse the situation. After the Mexican default it was clear that any plan designed to overcome paralysis in the financial market would have to go through the IMF. In the Brazilian case, the decision on timing of an agreement with the IMF was political, heavily influenced by the elections scheduled for late 1982. But moving initial negotiations from November back up to August would not have been enough to stop the drain on reserves or prevent a cutback on short-term credit.

One might ask whether banks would have reacted differently had Brazil gone to the IMF voluntarily as early as 1979. In Chapter 3 I discuss the IMF's policies—particularly what I see as its rigid methodological approach, which in practice makes such action on the part of debtor countries politically infeasible. It is not common practice for countries to pay a visit to the IMF voluntarily while reserves and access to the market are still open. Resources available from the IMF on short notice are so limited that announcement of an intended agreement does not send a useful signal to the financial community. When countries announce their intention to seek an agreement with the IMF, creditor banks usually cut voluntary lending and wait for the dust to settle.

As we know, the very short-term liquidity that Brazil did acquire was made possible by impromptu action on the part of the U.S. Treasury and the Bank for International Settlements (BIS)—an emergency action, since regular institutional mechanisms were lacking.[7] Despite this immediate aid, the later agreement with the IMF, and completion of the first rounds of debt rescheduling with the banks in February 1983, hemorrhage of interbank deposits did not end until June. The elapsed time illustrates how difficult it was to stop the self-perpetuating process of shrinking bank credits.

The question of default is even more controversial. It is often asked whether it would have been better to stop all payments immediately until rescheduling and agreement with the IMF had been accomplished. This action would have allowed us, hypothetically at least, to build up reserves and thus to increase our bargaining power.

As I will show in the following chapter, the existence in July 1982 of about $20 billion in short-term loans (trade credit and interbank deposits) of an informal nature, mostly self-liquidating, placed tight constraints on Brazil's room to maneuver. Since those credit lines had an average six-month maturity, to default on payment as of August clearly would have been unfavorable for Brazil: while the country would be holding back payments totaling about $5 billion over the next four months (the approximate amount of bank amortization and interest due), it would risk losing nearly $13 billion in credit lines.[8] No doubt the loss of short-term credit lines has not been greater for Brazil because the country showed a willingness to meet all payments due.

The need to preserve Brazilian banks overseas was another serious consideration. Unilateral action to freeze all interbank deposits would have had serious legal implications, and would have exposed Brazil's banks in other countries to the intervention of local monetary authorities. At the same time, Brazil immediately discarded the Mexican solution of nationalizing its financial system, which would have automatically minimized the risk of legal reprisals.

Given this line of thought, the key objective of Brazilian rescheduling was to turn the informal short-term loans outstanding into medium-term credit backed by formal commitment from the lender banks. In the meantime, and thanks to intensive one-to-one talks day after day, the collapse of Brazilian financial institutions abroad was prevented. The attempt to pressure foreign banks into renewing their deposits in Brazilian banks had obvious legal and practical limitations. The Central Bank of Brazil had no way of acting directly on foreign banks, especially minor regional ones; it had to rely on the goodwill of other central banks. The attitude of central banks in industrialized countries showed that they failed to grasp the seriousness of the situation. Some simply refused to exert any sort of moral pressure on their banks — a radically rigid interpretation of their legal powers of action. Since no liquidity rediscount mechanisms were available, the system's stability rested on the ability of major financial institutions to act. They did so purely to survive. As individual links in the extensive interbank deposit chain, they would be hit if the flow of renewals was interrupted.

The efficiency the system had shown when it had been operating under expansion was also evident during its contraction. Average

TABLE 1.6 Indebted Developing Countries – by Region: External Debt, by Class of Creditor, End of Year, 1977–86 (US$ billion)

	1977	1978	1979	1980	1981	1982	1983	1984	1985	1986
Indebted developing countries										
Total debt	332.4	398.3	470.9	565.0	660.5	747.0	790.7	827.7	865.3	896.5
Short-term	63.2	71.9	81.8	113.3	136.2	154.6	137.3	126.3	104.9	107.3
Long-term	269.2	326.5	389.1	451.7	524.3	592.4	653.4	701.3	760.3	789.2
Unguaranteed	55.1	57.8	68.7	83.0	104.4	114.2	108.8	110.5	104.1	102.5
Guaranteed	214.1	268.7	320.4	368.7	419.9	478.2	544.6	590.8	656.3	686.7
To official creditors	109.7	130.8	149.1	172.4	192.8	218.6	243.0	266.4	295.2	314.6
To financial institutions	72.9	99.6	130.2	154.0	182.1	208.5	249.8	271.2	304.1	313.4
To other private creditors	31.5	38.3	41.1	42.3	45.0	51.1	51.8	53.2	56.9	58.7

Source: World Bank

deposit maturities shrank at each renewal or were simply canceled. At one point deposits were dangerously concentrated in overnight operations, necessitating a daily effort for renewal. To keep the system going was a task calling for perseverance and steady nerves. Residual liquidity needs at the end of a day were covered by a limited number of major banks acting as a safety net.

The inherent fragility of such a scheme will be discussed in the next chapter. A unique combination of sophisticated electronics (computer printouts provided each branch of Brazilian banks throughout the world with data on deposits due over the following fifteen days) and endless hours of old fashioned ear-bending over the phone helped preserve our overseas financial system. Only later, after much pain and many scares, did the banks realize that such short-term loans were an integral component in financing the balance of payments.

Compulsory Adjustment

In October 1982 Brazil embarked on its first concrete adjustment experiment under the impossible conditions of a nonexistent financial market. It was a sad end to a growth strategy that had been launched precisely at the top of the recently created, thriving, and promising private market of long-term loans.

The troublesome external debts of developing countries became a key obstacle to stability of the world economy and particularly of the international financial system. It should be stressed that not all debtor countries found it equally difficult to clear the post-1982 hurdle. Clearly, the different development routes chosen by countries over the last years have made a big difference to them in the economic and social costs of the adjustment process.

The total external debt (short-, medium-, and long-term) of developing countries in late 1982 was estimated by the World Bank at $747 billion (Table 1.6). Private lenders accounted for 62 percent of the long-term debt, with the remainder divided between governments (24 percent) and multilateral institutions (14 percent). These figures illustrate the futility of government-to-government negotiation alone as a solution to the problem. All the players must be involved. As expected, the debt was heavily concentrated in non-oil-producing LDCs, which owed 82 percent of the total. If we look at the debtors in trouble which include countries that have accumulated arrears in debt service payments and those that have been forced to reschedule debt maturity dates or abide by a formal agreement with the IMF, we find that they account for about 60 to 70 percent of the LDC debt, or, around $500 billion.[9] The magnitude of the problem is clear: external debt is a serious problem, particularly in Latin America and Africa, where 85 percent of countries rated "in trouble" are located.

The external debt-to-GDP ratio is roughly the same for Latin America and Africa — around 50 percent. The difference is that Latin America has enjoyed greater access to private banks, which therefore account for a larger share of its debt. For this very reason, Latin America is more sensitive to interest rate fluctuations. Interest payments for Latin America in 1983 were estimated at 36 percent of exports. The major problem for African countries is their heavy reliance on a handful of commodity exports and the impact of general import restrictions on internal consumption of food.

In Asia, the Philippines stand out as being in a predicament similar to that of the major Latin American debtors, with a high interest-to-exports ratio and strained relations with banks and the IMF. South Korea has apparently managed to implement a voluntary adjustment program that has kept the doors of the financial market open.

A word about the Eastern European countries — East Germany, Rumania, and Hungary in particular. Market constraints were imposed on them following the Polish default. The external debt of those socialist bloc countries was estimated at $60 billion at year-end 1983, of which half was owed by the Polish — proof that the debt problem is not just one aspect of a broader issue that has been called the "crisis of capitalism." Centralized planning also has failed to prevent the collapse of nationalized economies.

One thing capitalist and socialist countries have in common is that the worst-hit economies are those that try to postpone their adjustment and finance their way out of disequilibrium. The use of this strategy by both east and west reflects the institutional rigidity that is associated with excessive state involvement in the economy. State intervention has forced both socialist and open-market countries into compulsory adjustment and an uncomfortable association with the IMF.

Results suggest that less state intervention, and the accompanying higher institutional flexibility, lowers the economic and social costs of overcoming the debt crisis. Chile is an exception, however: here, despite a notoriously market-oriented economy, the crisis hit with full force.[10]

Another key element in understanding why some developing countries were able to avoid the debt crisis is the emphasis placed on "export-oriented" versus "import substitution" in particular development strategies. Table 1.7 shows striking differences in debt service/export ratios in the 1977–1981 period among countries that rescheduled and those that did not: 181 percent versus 84 percent, respectively. The difference is particularly notable when comparing East Asia with Latin America.

The geopolitical consequences of seeing the external debt crisis as a problem particular to Latin America are easy to infer. However, the geographical concentration of the problem impedes comprehensive political action and weakens the bargaining power of each debtor country, turning the matter into a problem of negotiation (or confrontation) between Latin countries as a group and the United States as the heaviest lender.

Conclusions

This brief historical account contains many lessons for the future, as it documents the interrelationship between external debt imbalances and the world economy. From 1973 to 1983 a series of exogenous shocks, wide fluctuation of inflation rates, cycles of recovery interspersed with recession, and extreme variation of interest rates and major commodity prices were the headlines of the world economic story.

The impact of these events frequently has been underestimated. Persistent phenomena consistently have been interpreted as temporary, delaying compensatory action. Since 1984, the world economy has been pulled by the American recovery into a new cycle of expansion, this time at a relatively lower rate of inflation.

Is there reason to believe that a new round of self-sustained, non-

TABLE 1.7 Indebted Developing Countries: External Debt and Debt Service, 1977–86
(percent of exports of goods and services, except where otherwise noted)

	1977	1978	1979	1980	1981	1982	1983	1984	1985	1986
External debt										
Indebted developing countries	126.7	132.4	119.4	110.4	123.3	148.0	157.9	151.3	148.5	141.5
(US$ billions)	332.4	398.3	470.9	565.0	660.5	747.0	790.7	827.7	865.3	896.5
Africa	112.1	123.7	106.0	87.3	111.7	145.6	160.4	161.7	162.8	154.6
Asia	87.5	81.6	73.4	70.5	72.9	85.7	90.4	85.5	86.3	84.7
Europe	117.8	126.0	118.0	117.8	115.4	121.5	129.1	127.0	121.4	110.9
Non-oil Middle East	165.7	168.4	155.8	129.2	136.8	151.4	173.6	175.6	183.6	181.9
Western Hemisphere	191.8	215.0	194.7	183.3	210.9	270.7	294.1	280.0	269.6	257.6
Market borrowers	119.2	125.5	111.3	102.8	118.6	147.0	155.5	146.4	141.9	133.8
Official borrowers	149.3	163.0	152.8	156.8	179.5	219.2	244.7	257.8	267.1	268.0
Countries with recent debt-servicing problems	171.7	195.8	178.1	167.1	194.5	246.0	268.1	256.8	245.8	230.8
Countries without debt-servicing problems	95.3	91.9	81.6	73.6	78.3	91.1	97.0	94.2	95.8	93.6

Source: World Bank

inflationary growth will occur? If this important question can be answered in the affirmative, the expectation of a spontaneous correction of the external debt problem is justified, and there is no need to revise further the present terms of rescheduling.[11]

Yet, large uncertainties remain. The U.S. economy itself appears to have embarked lately on a trajectory of growth with indebtedness. Its indebtedness is not constrained by the balance of payments because the dollar is both a domestic and international currency. But this course involves a growing public deficit that, while it is moderate in relation to GDP, amounts to about 45 percent of personal savings.[12] To finance the debt, the United States requires a sufficiently positive interest rate differential to attract resources from abroad. Such an inflow of resources from abroad allows the country to sustain a substantial trade deficit, which in turn helps it to cut inflation. As a result, since 1984 the United States has turned from an important net capital exporter into a major net debtor.

Recently, U.S. vulnerability has become prominently visible. Sharp devaluation of the dollar since 1985 has not been enough to reverse the country's trade deficits, but dollar devaluation is exerting renewed inflationary pressures, which may lead to compensatory policies — perhaps a wrong mix of monetary and fiscal ingredients that will push up interest rates, contributing to a domestic recession and devastating the economies of debtor countries. Another serious risk is that lack of international coordination may increase the odds of a trade war.

Several developed countries also face the problem of economic reconversion or restructuring, necessitating phaseout of whole sectors of their economies not competitive with newcomers in the market: textiles, shoes, and steel in the United States; ships, agricultural products, and again steel in Europe; rice and meat production in Japan. Structural reform, economically unavoidable, might generate new export opportunities for developing countries, but faces strong political and social opposition at home. These essential changes are particularly difficult to undertake when unemployment is high. The historical relationship has been weakened between the expansion of international trade and the growth rate of major industrialized powers.

A retrospective look has shown that the 1982 debt problem was the result of a complex combination of internal and external factors.

The lack of an adequate international framework to deal with world economic crisis has become evident in recent years. A financial crash of unprecedented proportions has become thinkable. We shall see in the next chapters that orchestrated action, based on the principle of mutual responsibility, is a precondition to finding an orderly way out of the crisis.

2

Rescheduling and the Banks

On the afternoon of December 20, 1982, hundreds of bankers gathered at the Plaza Hotel in New York City to begin the formal rescheduling of Brazil's foreign debt. Brazilian government officials, representatives of the International Monetary Fund, private bankers: for most it was an unprecedented experience. They had been trained to deal with impersonal market forces. The direct, nervous contact of debtors and creditors was new to them. But as the market was no longer working, such meetings would soon become routine.[1]

Brazil's foreign debt came to $83.2 billion (Table 2.1). Eighty-four percent of this amount, $70 billion, was in medium- or long-term loans, and $13 billion in short-term loans (less than one year). Of that $13 billion, trade credit represented $9.2 billion, with the remainder being emergency loans negotiated in the final months of 1982.

Historically, most Brazilian debt has consisted of floating-rate loans from private banks. These accounted for 75 percent of the December 1982 total. Therefore, rescheduling necessarily meant negotiating with foreign private banks. Governmental credit was refinanced separately through the Club of Paris. Compared with that of other countries,

TABLE 2.1   Brazil: Structure of the External Debt *(US$ billion)*

	1982	1983	1984	1985	1986[a]
1. Total Debt	83.2	91.6	102.0	105.1	110.5
2. Nonregistered Debt	13.1	10.3	10.9	9.3	9.0
Registered Debt	70.1	81.3	91.1	95.8	101.5
3. Debt with foreign banks	58.7	64.3	70.7	68.5	n.a.
Debt with Brazilian banks	7.8	7.9	8.3	8.3	n.a.
Debt with nonbanking institutions	16.7	19.4	23.0	28.3	n.a.

Source: Central Bank of Brazil
[a] Preliminary data

Brazil's foreign debt profile was relatively favorable. We always have worked to spread out the due dates on loans. (In contrast, Mexico's default had been triggered by its concentration of short-term debt.) But the recent loan squeeze was more than care and management could handle.

The Plaza Hotel meeting was sought by Brazil upon realizing that net reserves after recent cutbacks in external loans would not be enough to meet impending obligations. Our international reserves totaled $6.9 billion in June 1982, less than the interest due in the second half of the year. Brazil had been draining its reserves in response to the deterioration in external conditions since 1979, but not even the earlier record level of reserves — $11.9 billion in 1978 — would have been enough to cover a sudden freeze on external loans. Such a level of reserves in 1982 would have bought some time, but would not have saved the country from rescheduling.

Under the December 1982 rescheduling agreement the nature of "new money" underwent profound changes. No longer was it tied to minimum investment levels as defined by debtor countries but rather to bank objectives: to make sure that interest was paid and to keep additional loans at levels substantially lower than the growth rate of their capital basis. New money became an "interest facility" to be obtained by the country under duress. The banks sought quickly to correct for their years of credit overexpansion.

Overdue payments continued to accrue throughout 1983, showing that despite the new arrangement and other negotiations the inflow of external funds to Brazil was still insufficient. An additional $3.5 billion had to be obtained, partially to cover the loss of short-term credit. These resources were negotiated together with $3 billion in new money that was required for liquidity in 1984. Under these tight conditions there was no private credit left for growth. On the contrary, net flow of financial resources became clearly negative, meaning that new credit, when available, fell short of the total interest bill.

As banks work to minimize their future LDC debt exposure, their strategy is not to lend money for buildup of reserves. The accumulation of reserves, critical to reopening financial markets, is made very difficult by these bank practices. For borrowers reserve gains must come from an improvement in the balance of trade, with occasional inflows from the IMF.

Quasi Syndication

The several months leading up to the Plaza Hotel meeting had witnessed a changeover from voluntary lending through the market to compulsory borrowing by LDCs under agreements through which the IMF persuaded private banks to grant the credit. This was a new role for the IMF, and this role was intended to ensure the minimum flow of external funds needed to finance the expected current account deficits of the LDCs. In the early years banks and governments alike considered an IMF agreement essential for rescheduling. As we shall see, this notion is slowly changing.[2] Such an agreement provides "institutional collateral" but it carries negative side effects — some over the short run, others with more lasting implications.

Brazil's agreement with the IMF opened the door to bridge loans from private banks ($2.4 billion), the Bank for International Settlements ($1.4 billion), and the U.S. Treasury ($1.8 billion). In the last quarter of 1982 there was almost no voluntary borrowing — just late disbursements from previous loans or import-related credit. The bridge loans arranged by the IMF generally matured in one year or less. They were vital: Brazil needed to avoid a major buildup in arrears. Outstanding payments would make rescheduling much more difficult; even without new arrears, a major sum of new money already was needed.

Before long the IMF's role had gone beyond persuasion, as banks were reluctant to commit resources in the needed amounts. The first compulsory syndication was to Mexico ($4 billion), the next to Brazil ($4.5 billion). These were concluded quickly in early 1983 as bankruptcy of the two countries appeared imminent. In Brazil's case, to reduce transaction costs the requirement to supply new money was limited to a group of large and medium-sized banks. A second Brazilian operation ($6.5 billion) took much longer because the attempt to increase the number of partners in these loans met with strong resistance from regional banks.

From a banker's point of view, the question is whether all banks will contribute their fair share of new money, an amount proportionate to the exposure they have accumulated over the years in a given country. How to determine what constitutes a "fair share" has not been settled; it is difficult both technically and politically. Just arriving at a date of reference from which to estimate the amount is a challenge. From the viewpoint of a borrower country, being compelled to raise resources from a large number of banks having varied expectations about the future of LDCs and about their own roles in international markets is particularly troublesome. The limitations posed by a diversity of domestic regulations make it worse.

As time goes by, conflicts tend to escalate between small and major institutions within lending nations. Small banks generally have less to lose by not participating in the effort to raise new money. Even major European and Asian banks, which operate in countries where regulations are more flexible, are weighing seriously the costs of the present quasi-syndication system, which requires ongoing pressure over smaller institutions. The banks have organized their actions in advisory or steering committees whose main task is to concentrate the decisionmaking process and conciliate the different interests of regional groups. As it stands, the system might be advocated as a contingency strategy to confront imminent shock waves; it should not be thought of as permanent. We are not dealing with just temporary disequilibria in our external accounts. These were corrected easily in the past through standby agreements, usually of one-year maturity.[3] The external and internal imbalances of developing countries are structural, and timing is a critical factor in keeping these balances in a workable range. Given the size of Brazil's foreign debt as well as that of many other LDCs, rescheduling will have to be carried out over many years. The time needed for correction of structural imbalances is certainly longer than the life of the current IMF adjustment model. So is the time until LDCs can expect to resume voluntary borrowing in financial markets. Industrialized countries and banks are counting on long-term intervention by the IMF. With the required time frame for adjustment being very long, the question now is what pattern the old love-hate relationship among developing countries, banks, and the IMF should take place. The current shape with stringent conditionalities is unacceptable to debtor countries, and unworkable in the long run.

The basic issue is how to make the transition to a new stage of unsupervised rescheduling, whereby banks could go back to relying on their own assessment of a country's performance instead of looking for a green light from the IMF.

An alternative scenario would be to have the World Bank replace the IMF to a certain extent as institutional collateral to ensure minimum levels of external loans. Expansion of co-financing (or joint financing), whereby the World Bank uses resources from private banks to augment its own limited capital, may be a useful compromise between the current system and the ideal, still far in the future—i.e., market resumption. The key to this scheme lies in the enhanced flexibility of conditionalities that will result if the World Bank takes a more active part. The World Bank also sets requirements for borrowing, but it does not require such formalities as a letter of intent: historically, the role it has played has been more suitable for dealing with structural problems underlying foreign debt than for adjustment issues. Chapter 3 will discuss how the banks view the IMF's role in such a transition.

Market Rules, Nonmarket Situation

The current renegotiation exercise has been a case of applying market rules to a nonmarket situation. Until very recently, both the costs charged under rescheduling and the compulsory system of raising additional funds, described above as quasi syndication,[4] have been carried out as though the market were operating. In the past, borrowing in the market had two main objectives: to assure the rollover of amortization payments and to raise enough new money to finance investment projects. Spreads and fees were set to reflect relative country risk, which was closely associated with the magnitude of loans required (mirroring the country's overall economic standing), the ratio of public to private loans, and the existence of tax credits. In Brazil, for example, spreads were raised to allow for increasingly greater volumes of funds in the market and to help cover high current account deficits. Brazil has chosen to accept the spread increase as inevitable while preserving its debt profile and holding its borrowing to eight-year minimum maturities. Other countries have reduced such spreads artificially and taken in short-term loans, increasing their external vulnerability.

Under the new debt rescheduling terms, a formal distinction was drawn between amortization and new money. For Brazil these two categories were designated Projects I and II during the first rescheduling round (1983), and Projects A and B in the second round (1984). Refinancing the amortization was broadly accepted by the banks as unavoidable, because prompt repayment of principal could not be expected under normal conditions, let alone at the onset of a liquidity crunch.

The process was no longer voluntary, of course; all banks holding 1983 maturities were forced to refinance the amount due automatically, under the same market terms prevailing before the Mexican default. The only difference was the extension of the grace period from two-and-a-half to five years. Amortization was handled under two major guidelines: all financial institutions with assets in the country were included in the scheme; and once started the process would be automatic and could not be stalled by a unilateral decision by any lender. Amortization is the only area of external financing in which the decisionmaking process is controlled by the debtor countries.

In practice, the process of compulsorily rolling over amortizations follows its course despite eventual problems in the implementation of adjustment programs. This was the first area in which rescheduling without the IMF was made possible. The best illustration is the Brazilian experience. In 1983, when the original IMF program had to be revised, extended fund facility (EFF) and new money disbursements had to be stopped, but the compulsory rollover of amortization proceeded, with no legal objections by the creditors.[5] By the same token, since January 1985, when negotiations with the IMF broke off, Brazil has continuously refinanced amortizations falling due at a lower cost but with shorter maturities. The banks' attitude in this case can be explained not just as a passive and fatalistic acceptance of circumstances, but also by the ease with which they managed to accommodate the rescheduled principal in their books.

The gap between what the bankers see as their level of risks after rescheduling, and what the LDCs see as their minimum external financial needs will be very difficult to close, and is a key issue throughout th..s book.

Bank Charges for Rescheduling

Loan costs under rescheduling were set to approximate the figures that would prevail under market conditions. The estimated spread on the external interest rate, the Labor Interbank Offering Rate (LIBOR) was 2.125 in 1983, 2.0 in 1984, and 1.125 in 1985–86. Additional fees and commissions were charged at approximately market levels.[6] In some instances — and Mexico is a good example — spreads were higher after the first reschedulings than before the default. (Table 2.2)

When a country fails to pay on its loans, the idea that spreads should reflect risks has no meaning. Either the risks are so great that all loans would be called off (equivalent to infinitely high spreads in a market context), or margins should reflect an entirely new set of circumstances — a restructured economy. In the latter case, *expected* risks become the relevant factor, and they can not be explained solely by a country's past performance.

During the transition period, when the ground is being set for a resumption of equilibrium in the economy, spreads should reflect transaction costs rather than arbitrary assessments of risk. This type of calculation leads to a significant decline in short-run bank returns, but such a decline is unavoidable one way or another in adjusting the financial system.

TABLE 2.2   Brazil: Rescheduling Terms

	Phase 1 (1983)	Phase II (1984)	Phase III (1985/1986)
Short-term[a]	US$ 15.0 billion	US$ 15.0 billion	US$ 15.0 billion
Amortization	US$ 4.7 billion	US$ 5.3 billion	US$ 17.9 billion
New Money	US$ 4.4 billion	US$ 6.5 billion	none
Maturity	8 years	9 years	6 years
Grace Period	2.5 years	5 years	3 years
Spread Over Labor	2.125%	2.0%	1.125%–1.225%
Flat Fee	1.5%	1.0%	none
Commitment Fee	1.0%	1.0%	none

Source: Central Bank
[a] Trade-related and interbank

Insistence on setting an artificial price for rescheduled loans as though market were fully operational has been one of the most unfavorable aspects of the debt rescheduling process. Even in the August 1984 multiyear Mexican rescheduling, bank spreads, despite some reduction, remained above pre-default market levels. Only more recently, in the 1986 Mexican negotiations and 1987 Argentinian and Philippinian ones, was there a sharp decline in spreads, which reached 0.8125 above the LIBOR.

To impose high financial costs is not common banking practice when dealing with corporations that get into trouble. It does, however, show how limited the bargaining power of debtor countries has been until recently; it also reveals implicity how sensitive the overall profits of the financial system are to any slight change in the return on financial assets invested in developing countries.

Short-Term Loans

Short-term funds are like uneven pieces — hard to fit into the debt puzzle. In the case of Brazil there are two kinds of short-term credit: trade-related and interbank lines. Since the international and domestic financial markets began to interact in the late 1960s, Brazilian authorities have been very concerned with the country's external debt profile. Minimum maturities were defined for the country to take maximum advantage of long-term loans that are available within prevailing market liquidity conditions. As most such external resources are geared to fixed assets, there also has been an effort to reconcile the physical investment profile with loan maturities. At the time of the Mexican shock, for instance, minimum maturities for syndicated operations were eight years, with a four-year grace period. In contrast to many other countries, Brazil did not seek shorter maturities to achieve a spread reduction. Nor was our policy overflexible, like that of Argentina or Chile, where free rein was given to financial flows without any restriction on maturity. Such a policy fosters the emergence of destabilizing movements whenever exchange expectations suddenly change. We should not forget that the triggering mechanism for the Mexican default was precisely the accumulation of short-term funds to finance growing current account deficits.

Only when crisis hit did Brazil resort to short-term loans to finance the current account deficit; not until the nonmarket situation arose did we seek emergency bridge loans. So in the Brazilian case the growth in short-term debt did not result from a deliberate policy of balance-of-payments financing; it was the natural outcome of international trade expansion and the external projections of our domestic financial system. The increasing share of manufactured goods among total exports—$14.5 billion in 1984, 53 percent of the total—has boosted the demand for short-term credit. On the import side, the rising oil bill, particularly in the period 1978–1982, inevitably led to more intensive use of short-term funds. Trade loans reached $9.3 billion in late 1982, while medium- and long-term debts rose to $70.2 billion. These figures seemed quite reasonable considering the overall volume of Brazilian foreign trade.

Short-term loans bring great vulnerability. First of all, these are by definition unregistered debts, until recently informal ones. Second, they are self-liquidating. Even marginal reductions in short-term credit have a disproportionate impact on external liquidity by introducing an unfavorable differential between accounting figures and actual cash inflows, both in exports and imports. Brazil was particularly vulnera-

ble because about two-thirds of the overall trade line was directed toward
financing oil purchases.

Between August 1982 and the first quarter of 1983, Brazil lost $2
billion to $3 billion in trade lines, with devastating effects on its exter-
nal liquidity. Given its unregistered and informal character, this credit
weighed heavily in the Brazilian government's decision not to default
formally. At the same time, stabilization of these credit lines became
one of the key targets of rescheduling. In mid-1983, Brazil's loans finally
settled at around $10 billion. Meanwhile, direct credit lines were
obtained from oil suppliers to take advantage of market conditions
favoring importer countries.

Brazil Centralizes Exchange Flows

Upon the stabilization of short-term funds, it became possible for Brazil
to concentrate the control of exchange flows in its Central Bank. That
August 1983 action ensured a rationing of foreign exchange and eliminated the risk of interrupting the supply of oil and other goods and
services vital to the Brazilian economy. Although centralization meant
a monopoly on exchange operations (and therefore could only be
enforced temporarily), it strengthened the country's bargaining power
significantly vis-à-vis the banks. In practice it allowed for the informal
suspension of interest payments on medium- and long-term loans and
a remarkable improvement in the Central Bank's foreign cash position.
It also helped strengthen the pressure on foreign banks to provide additional new money as the only way to avoid having their Brazilian loans
classified as nonperforming.[7] Centralization of the exchange flows
was a *de facto* undeclared and undetermined default. It was phased
out only after new funds were released by the banks and the IMF in
March 1984.

Centralization helps explain the fast recovery of Brazil's foreign
exchange by the second half of 1983. In 1984 trade lines were consolidated and became a firm commitment by the banks over a one-year
period. Since then these lines have been extended over shorter periods, even without an overall rescheduling agreement, provided that
interest payments are maintained. Trade lines may be an area where

voluntary borrowing can be restored over time; it might be done concurrently with the expected growth of foreign trade among the LDCs.

Three years later, in 1987, Brazil again suspended interest payments on long-term credit to private banks, this time to avoid the complete exhaustion of international reserves. Instead of providing new money to reestablish interest flows, the banks have chosen to increase loan loss provisions. By mid-1987, this boost in reserves has reached $12.9 billion for American banks only. This may be interpreted as a turning point in the compulsory refinancing strategy that prevailed from 1982 to 1986.

Interbank Deposits

The internationalization of the finance systems of major newly industrialized countries such as Brazil is a direct consequence of the development of a dollar-based world financial market and the proliferation of money centers. It seemed natural for private and state LDC banks with substantial capital to locate branches abroad and compete directly for external resources. Selection of participating LDC banks was made by the central banks of host countries.[8] By 1962 sixteen Brazilian banks operated abroad, with 104 branches and deposits of $10 billion.

Deposits in those banks were a natural target for host country banks as they strove to reduce their LDC credit overexposure. In such cases interbank credit lines are particularly vulnerable to discontinuation, as they traditionally have been considered "residuals," temporary resources that might or might not be renewed on maturity. Under market conditions, the maturity of such deposits ranges from one day to a year, with the median at six months. Any change in expectations is likely to cause a maturity squeeze, resulting in a dangerous pattern of overnight operations. Accompanying the Mexican shock there was a simultaneous net drain (i.e., interbank deposits liquidations outnumbered renewals), rise in costs, and reduction in average deposit maturities. In the four months following the Mexican default, Brazilian banks lost $4 billion in interbank deposits. It is impossible to reduce loan assets rapidly enough to compensate for a sudden outflow of such magnitude. That would be particularly true for major state banks whose activities are mostly directed to long-term financing. Private banks would have more flexibility, for a large part of their assets would be tied to trade operations. The problem was magnified in Brazilian banks by the heavy concentration of loans in Latin America. At the same time, through lost interbank deposits, a significant share of their assets became illiquid and no longer generated returns.

A direct relationship was thus established between the performance of a country's balance of payments and the fate of its banks. The converse also applied: should any Brazilian bank collapse, the chances would be substantially reduced of ensuring a minimum inflow to the country of external funds. It was crucial to keep Brazilian banks afloat in the storm. The interbank deposit drain became a *de facto* drain on the external accounts themselves. During the last months of 1982 we lived in a Kafkaesque world in which bridge loans painfully negotiated with the largest international banks, governments, and multilateral institutions were used not to improve the country's liquidity, but to support Brazilian banks overseas.

The loan and deposit behavior of international banks did not improve significantly, despite the 1982 rescheduling agreement and approval in February 1983 of the adjustment program by the IMF board. In fact, some of the smaller institutions saw rescheduling as a stimulus to hasten reductions in short-term credit lines in order to offset anticipated increases in long-term exposure.

The drain on interbank deposits could not be overcome without leadership from major central banks. Yet some of these banks were not renewing their own deposits in Brazilian banks. Lack of coordinated action, intervention ill suited to the emergency, conflicting regional viewpoints — all these contributed to a delay in the action required to stop the drain. The situation was particularly complex for Brazil, both because our overseas branches were large and because our policy was against state ownership of the banking system. The possibility of a unilateral freeze on deposits was limited by the risk of legal reprisals. So Project IV faced a nearly impossible challenge: to reverse the expectations of 700 banks worldwide with only the help of a few large banks and some of the central banks.

It was a difficult and hazardous task. No central bank agreed to open an automatic rediscount window to cover liquidity gaps, even

TABLE 2.1   **Long-term Loans Made by Private Financial Institutions**
            (US$ billion)

Source: World Bank

for the very short run. We couldn't help but notice the difference between the way the needs of our banks in the United States were handled and the rescue of Continental Illinois Bank.[9]

Total collapse was avoided only by a "safety net," whereby major banks covered the residual funds required at the end of each day. It was a shaky system, because the rollover of deposits concentrated in the overnight market was totally open to view, reminding observers daily of how uncertain the market was and making it impossible to restore deposits to historic levels. A substantial number of small and medium-sized regional financial institutions pulled out most of their deposits. The remaining banks carried such weight in the market and were so deeply invested in Brazil that they could not get away. In July

1983 an agreement was reached to freeze interbank deposits for one year. It was implemented in early 1984.

The debt crisis had toppled another banking myth. No longer can interbank deposits be considered random residuals; not, at least, when they are tied into the support of long-term loans.

Capital Outflow

The Amex Bank Review has estimated that for nine countries—(Argentina, Brazil, Chile, Ecuador, Mexico, Peru, Turkey, Venezuela, and Yugoslavia) the additional term debt supplied by the banks after the crisis ($9.2 billion) was completely offset by the cut in short-term and standby lines ($1.3 billion and $7.9 billion, respectively).[10] If interest payments are added ($34.1 billion), we arrive at a net outflow of $34 billion from these LDCs. A similar picture is seen in the balance of payments for 1982–1986 in Latin America as a whole: a net outflow of resources, $132 billion, representing 25 percent of the region's exports.

This abrupt transformation of debtor countries into net exporters of capital is one of the most important features of the recent crisis, and it has important long-term implications for the region's development. It came about as the result of the sharp curtailment of credit to these countries combined with an acceleration of interest rates. Unfortunately, real rates of interest have remained unusually high for more than five years, and no one knows when the United States will meet its own performance criteria as to the public deficit.

The meaning of this net outflow of capital depends on whether it is looked at from the short-run (adjustment) viewpoint or from the standpoint of development. From the *adjustment* viewpoint, the relevant constraint is the size of the current account deficit to be financed. The only sustainable trend is one in which the total net inflow of resources (including risk capital) is at least equal to and preferably higher than the expected current account deficits. It can be argued that, given the rigidity in external interest rates, a financial outflow is not only inevitable but even desirable, since gross borrowing must be cut if one is to reduce the pace of external indebtedness. If, however, the goal is a positive flow of credits (forgetting for a moment any supply limitation), we would have to accept a higher rate of total debt growth—i.e., deducting reserve variations—though not necessarily of the net debt position. In Brazil, for example, a zero net financial flow in 1983–1986 would mean a substantial gain in reserves for identical trade performance.

For a clearer picture of this profound structural change in the financial markets, let us compare Brazil's 1982–1984 period with the first oil shock (1974–1976). As mentioned in Chapter 1, external disequilibrium, when measured by the ratio of current account deficit to GDP, was larger following the 1974 oil shock (6.8 percent) than in 1982 (5.2 percent). However, since financial markets were functioning normally in 1974 and interest rates were falling, adjustment was gradual and was associated with a significant net inflow of credits ($44 billion). In sharp contrast, after 1982 the combination of financial market constriction and high rates of interest forced a more rapid, compulsory adjustment linked to a substantial net outflow of resources. During the period 1982–1984, the net transfer of capital reached $17.4 billion, equivalent to 25 percent of total exports and 2.5 percent of GDP. The situation has deteriorated further in 1985–1986: despite the fall in interest rates, there has been no agreement over new credits from private banks, and this has led to a relative increase in net transfers abroad. This is a critical factor in explaining Brazil's February 1987 repayment moratorium. The financial squeeze inevitably led to a pattern of adjustment with recession, in contrast to the mere slowdown in growth rate that followed the 1974 oil shock (Table 2.3).

It seems clear that the strategy of international banks is to shrink as far as they can the already reduced provision of additional credit to countries that have rescheduled their debt. Net long-term credit from banks to LDCs has been cut from $91 billion in 1981 to $3 billion in 1986. Banks will continue lending the minimum that will assure full payment of interest, without serious concern for the countries' development needs. The only hope for filling the gap between the goals of debtor countries and the banks' own targets for adjustment, lies in official resources as yet tentatively defined. Looking at total net bank loans to non-oil-producing LDCs, we find not just an abrupt contraction in overall volume, but also a sharp drop in the banks' relative share of financing available to those countries, from 65 percent throughout 1974–1980 to a mere 4 percent in 1986.

TABLE 2.3   Comparison of Two External Shocks *(US$ billion)*

| Years | Trade Balance | Current Account | | Net Financial Flow[a] | Interest Payments | Net Absorption (+) or Transfer (−) of Resources |
		Absolute Values	As % of GDP			
1974	− 4.7	− 7.1	6.8	5.3	− 0.6	4.7
1975	− 3.5	− 6.7	5.4	5.3	− 1.5	3.8
1976	− 2.2	− 6.0	4.0	5.9	− 1.8	4.1
1982	0.8	− 14.7	5.2	5.2	− 11.3	− 6.1
1983	6.3	− 7.6	3.0	2.8	− 9.5	− 6.7
1984	13.1	+ 0.5	0	5.7	− 10.2	− 4.5
1985	12.5	+ 0.3	0	2.8	− 9.7	− 7.1
1986	9.5	− 2.8	1.1	3.0	− 9.1	− 6.1

[a] Defined as total loans plus suppliers less amortizations. Figures for 1982/84 do not include IMF loans.

Between 1982 and 1986 banks managed to stave off losses while they waited for debtor countries to adjust and for world economic conditions to improve so that full debt service payments could be resumed at current costs. Such a scenario has always seemed unrealistic. Despite improvement in the world economy, and substantial reductions in current account deficits, there was no significant change in key indicators of creditworthiness, such as the debt service/export ratio.[11] Self-sustained adjustment will require structural changes such as export diversification and import substitution, both of which require a long period of time.

Social and political constraints are making it increasingly difficult to sustain the present system of adjustment with recession or slow growth. The unilateral suspension of interest payments by Brazil and the formal internalization of losses by leading U.S. banks in 1987 should not have come as a surprise.[12] These events represent the beginning of a new and more realistic stage of debt negotiation that will force a deeper change in rescheduling terms and procedures. In particular, the cost of borrowing is becoming a key issue for negotiation.

Clearly, the problem goes beyond the share of interest payments represented by bank spreads. The use of conventional interest rates such as the six-month LIBOR and Prime introduces wide variability in a country's external cash flow, which cannot be fully offset by internal action. The combination of a larger stock of debt and abnormally high real interest rates has made interest payment the most critical factor in the external accounts of most debtor countries. In 1984, a year in which Brazil's exports showed outstanding performance, net interest payments mounted to nearly $10.6 billion, or 39 percent of overseas revenue. So, within the present framework, unless quantities and prices are set simultaneously, no one can talk of a self-financing current account deficit—a major target of IMF programs—even for a period as brief as one year.

The ideal pattern of short-run adjustment for LDCs would be to have zero net financial outflow for a given trade account, reached not by an increase in gross borrowing, but by interest rate flexibility. The picture would then change dramatically, showing much quicker improvement in the current account deficit, an accumulation of reserves, and a slowdown in the expansion of external debt.

But the real world is not so bright. Short-run adjustment is not a voluntary choice made by countries in an ideal process of cost minimization. As a matter of fact, adjustment is compulsory and made under specified external conditions: availability of funds and interest rates. Under these circumstances, the trade balance is residual: you must generate whatever trade surplus is necessary to cope with the external constraints. Your relative effectiveness will depend on whether trade surpluses are being generated through export expansion or artificially, through import reduction. In the short to medium run, this pattern of adjustment will dominate the country's growth possibilities, having a greater effect than the major cut in external savings that accompanies a change in direction of net financial flows.

Notice also that the stepwise approach followed by banks in a non-market situation may lead to a perverse process whereby successful adjustment in any given year—measured by greater-than-projected current account improvement and reserve accumulation—may reduce the banks' incentive to provide additional financing the following year. This scenario reflects the conflicting objectives of banks and countries: from the viewpoint of the financial system, adjustment means a reduction in the rate of increased exposure, ideally to the point where no new financing is needed. From the country's viewpoint, the best indication of successful adjustment may be the rapid accumulation of reserves. It is clear that exogenous elements such as the IMF and the governments of developed countries will have to enter the picture to assure a more equitable and efficient outcome.

The change that has taken place in debtor countries from capital importing to net capital exporting makes their long-term development still more difficult. The trend must be reversed. Even though external savings were never a very significant element in Brazil's overall economy (3.5 percent of GDP in 1970–1980), they were extremely important to our growth.[13] A large part of external borrowing was directly associated with fixed capital investment. Only the external resources borrowed through Resolution 63 could be used as working capital. Furthermore, we must take into account the indirect effects on growth of the interconnectedness among financial capital, imported fixed capital, and technological change.

Even with the orthodox view that money is, after all, fungible and that the marginal rate of investment out of external resources cannot be very different from that of domestic funds, continuation of the current outflow is likely to mean a permanent reduction in Brazil's growth rate. Such potential loss may be offset in some measure by gains from improved allocation of resources or higher productivity. But in the long run, continuing net transfer of financial resources out of the country is bound to curtail the renewal of real product growth.

In summary, both short-term and long-term analyses point out that the present rescheduling strategy should not be seen as a permanent solution. Banks and industrialized governments are now beginning to understand that. Thought and action will be required to avoid the proliferation of unilateral actions.

Impact on Real Income

The past two years of economic adjustment in Brazil have been rather painful, the shift from market borrowing to rescheduling neither smooth nor efficient. The aggregate result masks the distortions and inequities of the strategy: at its core is shortsightedness by the industrialized countries, which simplistically interpreted the situation as a transitory liquidity crisis. The reduction in foreign financing has been more severe than could be justified even from the strict viewpoint of external imbalances. There has been a prolonged period of uncertainty, particularly damaging to our private sector. In the years 1982 and 1983 real output and employment plummeted to historically unprecedented levels.

All of Latin America has felt the crunch, not just as a slowdown in development but as an absolute shrinkage in the nations' economies. Per capita income decreased 7.5 percent regionwide between 1982 and 1986. Even assuming optimistically that growth can be resumed and sustained at a 5 percent rate in real terms, the 1980 per capita income level will not be reached again before 1990. The 1980s will have been a loss from the viewpoint of Latin American development.

Even to restore development by the 1990s, a minimum level of external resources necessary for Brazil or any other LDC needs to be established as a matter of international economic policy. Three critical matters must be faced in defining a long-term strategy of adjustment with growth:

1. The need to reduce uncertainty, which requires a stronger link between short-run adjustment and long-term development objectives.

2. The political impossibility of LDCs accepting a long-term arrangement whereby hard-won trade surpluses are still accomplished by the slow accumulation of reserves while the net flow of capital continues to be outward.

3. The need for lenders to accept that LDCs must be allowed to run a certain level of current account deficit and that they require an adequate level of capital inflow to sustain economic development.

The problem varies widely within Latin America: Peru's economy has been slowly collapsing for a long time; the recent crisis was just a trough in the country's long-term trend of retrogression. Since 1976,

Peru has shown a decline in per capita real product. Its GDP fell by
12 percent in 1983 alone. Chile has accumulated an external debt that
is now higher than GDP, and it is successfully finding a way out of the
crisis through liberalization of its economy. Argentina is faced with a
dangerous squeeze between inflation and economic stagnation, particularly in the industrial sector, and seeks greater economic integra-
tion with Brazil. The other two leading economies in the region, Brazil
and Mexico, have likewise experienced recession of unprecedented
severity. Brazilian per capita income fell by 5.5 percent in 1983 and
Mexican GDP growth was minus 5 percent. More recently (1984–1986)
these two countries have shown signs of economic reactivation, in some
measure a reflection of the U.S. economic recovery. Mexico remains
vulnerable to fluctuations in oil prices, while Brazil's future is endan-
gered by hyperinflation. Venezuela and Colombia are medium-sized
economies less affected by the debt crisis, but they have not yet found
the way to steady growth.

A consistent level of external finance must be a key element in a
more realistic debt strategy. A fundamental objective must be to reduce
the current level of uncertainty in world financial markets and to ensure
a quicker return to self-sustained growth among debtor countries. To
reduce uncertainty implies breaking the automatic relationship between
internal adjustment and external finance. Over time, external and internal adjustment do tend to converge. But they will not behave har-
moniously, quarter after quarter, as implied in current rescheduling
agreements. Instead, over a time-span of at least a year, debtor nations
should be allowed to count on access to the previously agreed upon
level of external finance, whatever may happen to internal targets. After
that, new financing should be negotiated, taking into consideration
the overall performance of the economy, external and internal. This
flexibility could be introduced with respect to IMF disbursements: one
quarter is too short a period for evaluation of a country's performance,
particularly too short to trigger a squeeze on external liquidity. This
possibility is discussed in the next chapter. Also, uncertainty would
be reduced by protecting a country's cash flow from the variability of
external interest rates. This may be achieved by different methods, including an automatic clause for additional new money to compensate
for unforeseen interest rate fluctuations or other external shocks.

A More Permanent Solution

Partial interest capitalization offers a more permanent solution. It would reduce the need for time-consuming and inefficient quasi syndications. The amount of interest to be refinanced would be based on the differential between current levels and equilibrium levels, the latter defined as the long-term expected interest rate. Regulatory and legal constraints in some countries may be overcome by formal assurance of full repayment at the agreed maturity.[14]

This concept implies two definitions of long-term equilibrium: one with reference to the inflation rate and then another to real interest rates. Whenever the current behavior of either variable is basically different from equilibrium figures, the differential would be capitalized automatically—that is, refinanced.

In practical terms, the long-term equilibrium interest rate could be pegged to the average LIBOR for the period 1960–1980, estimated at 2 percent in real terms or 6 percent nominally (i.e., including inflation). In the 1983–1987 period, the market interest rate averaged 9 percent. Application of the partial capitalization principle would reduce interest paid to the banks by roughly one-third. Excluding multilateral organizations and interest on short-term credits loans, Brazil's interest bill would fall from an average of $9.6 billion to around $6.5 billion. That would be equivalent to an inflow of new money on the order of $3 billion per year, not too different from the compulsory jumbo loans raised during the period 1983–1984 or from the requirements estimated for 1987–88.

The true difference between partial interest capitalization and syndicated loans lies precisely in not having to pay out $3 billion instead of borrowing compulsively the same amount. Under the new strategy, decisionmaking would shift from the international banks to the developing countries. It is this shift of control that may be the most sensitive issue, and might explain the resistance of some major institutions, particularly in the United States. As we will see, mechanisms may be devised to accommodate the impact of such a scheme on bank earnings and thereby not affect the stability of the financial system.

The reason for resistance to this plan is primarily strategic: refinancing interest together with amortization would make the rescheduling process almost automatic. The computers of debtor countries' central banks would replace the notorious advisory committees of lender banks, decreasing the influence of private banks over the choice of adjustment strategy by debtor countries. Partial interest capitalization would also reduce indirectly the IMF's margin for maneuver. This would be true especially in countries that could reach a new stage of self-sustained growth, relying only on the volume of resources implicitly generated by the partial capitalization of interest and by the regular contributions from multilateral organizations.

Two other features of this new framework stand out. First, it would insulate debtor countries from the effects of U.S. anti-inflationary policy. This side effect of U.S. domestic policy is not just a political embarrassment for that country's administration, in practice it also curtails the discretion of the Federal Reserve in monetary policy because of the constant threat posed by potential default by debtor countries — particularly in Latin America — to the U.S. financial system. This helps explain why, in the first months of 1984, when anxiety was at a peak on Wall Street because of the uncertainty brought about by the Brazilian and Argentine situations, Federal Reserve chairman Paul Volcker began to pressure the banks in support of the capitalization theory. Preston Martin, vice chairman of the Federal Reserve, and Anthony Salomon, president of the Federal Reserve Bank in New York, raised the issue again. It would have been more comfortable for Volcker to implement the eventually unavoidable monetary squeeze to offset the U.S. fiscal expansion without having to worry about the backlash caused by an increase in interest rates to be imposed on debtor countries. However, the idea of capitalizing interest remained dormant for lack of enthusiasm by the U.S. administration, lack of concerted action among Latin countries, and because favorable conditions in the world economy in 1984–86 had brought about windfall gains in the trade balances of debtor countries.

In addition to its intrinsic advantages, the partial capitalization of interest might be an important transition tool in order to extend the rescheduling concept — so far limited to the flow of resources — into a new stage that also includes the stock of the debt. This transition would be achieved naturally through the strong stimulus provided by the differential generated between the expected returns on financial and real assets. The advantages of such a gradual and voluntary change are so ample and self-evident that they would fully justify any involvement of resources from developed countries in the financial equalization mechanisms described below. It is obvious that while loan payment to banks are kept current based on the high real interest rates that prevail in the financial market, there will be little stimulus for these institutions to turn part of their loan assets into equity capital. However, if interest rates were reduced via rescheduling, risk capital investments would become relatively more attractive for financial institutions concerned with preserving profitability.[15] Therefore, it would be up to developing countries to lay out internal policies that would render the transformation of loans into capital more attractive. Under such an arrangement, mechanisms should be built in to make sure the conversion will not lead to unnecessary takeover of local domestic corporations.[16]

Debt/equity swaps are more attractive to banks now that LDC difficulties in maintaining a steady flow of debt service are becoming evident after five years of conventional rescheduling. Chile has successfully worked out more than $1 billlion of swaps since 1985. Mexico approved legislation allowing such conversions in 1986, and Argentina is experimenting with a new program in 1987. Brazil, after playing a pioneer role in this area during 1982–1984, has limited its involvement by legislation on a case-by-case basis, which may soon become more flexible. As the trend of writing off Latin American assets that was initiated by small regional banks and is now reaching the large Japanese and U.S. banks becomes general, the attractiveness of debt/equity swaps will be still greater.

Contrary to what is often said, therefore, partial interest capitalization is not just another trick to postpone a true solution to the external debt crisis. It is a rational path to a definitive solution: with less uncertainty and better liquidity, adjustment could be achieved in a framework of economic growth. Debt stock would readjust slowly and gradually until a new level of self-sustained equilibrium were achieved. All of this can be accomplished without grandiose schemes involving the creation of new international organizations.[17]

The impact of this change on banks' current earnings will vary from country to country and will have to be dealt with case by case.

Over the last years many banks have accumulated enough reserves to allow the absorption of a transitory fall in interest revenues without needing any special relief mechanism. In some cases, a special rediscount scheme of a broader nature, such as an interest facility, may be required to assure the stability of the financial system. The basic principle of such a fund would be the same as the one underlying the "oil facility" established by the IMF in 1974 to refinance the differential between current prices—distorted by OPEC's action—and what was considered to be a sort of long-term equilibrium price for oil. What the interest facility and the oil facility have in common is the need to reconcile bank earnings, which are based on current rates, with the flow of payments from the debtor countries, which would be calculated using the shadow rate. The new interest facility could be funded by either private or official sources. One alternative would be to use new allocations of special drawing rights (SDRs). Some losses will have to be absorbed by the banks. Basically, these losses reflect the adjustment process operating within the framework of the international finance system.

This alternative is, of course, superior to unexpected unilateral suspension of payments by debtor countries, now forcing large banks to increase reserves drastically and to reduce current earnings. In contrast, by allowing for a sustainable adjustment by developing countries, the new system would minimize the risk of capital losses, releasing resources from the banks that would otherwise be frozen under legal reserve requirements.

The partial capitalization of interest has much the same effect as a revolving fund repaid over a sufficiently long period of time. By definition, current rates will fluctuate over the long run around the equilibrium level, and the differences—both positive and negative—will cancel each other out. Debtor countries would automatically capitalize the positive differential (when current rates were higher than shadow rates), which later would be paid out of the extra earnings that the banks would realize when current rates were below the equilibrium level. In this sense there is no real resource transfer from industrialized countries either to the banks or to debtor nations, just a turnover of financial resources.

In any case, as suggested by Dr. Eric Hoffmeyer of the Central

Bank of Denmark, some investment of public resources from industrialized countries may be justified. Developing countries are not only transferring net resources abroad, they are also indirectly paying income tax to the United States through the differential between pre-tax and after-tax interest rates.[18] These fiscal resources theoretically could be reoriented to support the interest facility.

Another variation on the partial capitalization scheme is to issue dollar-indexed bonds as a substitute for current private bank debt. The fraction of interest payment to be capitalized would be represented by the dollar inflation. Countries would pay only a real rate of interest, which would reduce the payment burden on a cash flow basis, rather than on a discounted basis. The appeal of this proposal lies in the possibility of eventually transferring some of the new bonds to nonbanking institutions, such as pension funds, thus diminishing the need for government refinancing schemes.

Other new proposals are being developed from the reality of the newly created secondary debt market, where the prices of different country debts are quoted. The generalized trend by private banks in constituting loan-loss reserves may allow the exchange of current debt with new assets, such as long-term bonds, whose total value would amount to only a fraction of the original commitment based on the secondary market discounts. This would represent a substantial reduction in the debt stock itself. The incentive for the voluntary exchange would be the full assurance of payment on interest and principal through the organization of a "sinking fund"—either with the IMF, the World Bank, or even a creditor government's central bank—in which a fraction of the debtor countries' export earnings would be systematically allocated for the specific purpose of servicing the debt. Of course, in this case, interest payment would correspond to the full market LIBOR. The spreads in the new debt would vary proportionally to the relative size of the sinking fund. This approach would gain an extra stimulus if the proposal currently being discussed in the U.S. Congress, under the leadership of Senator Bradley, to create an Institute of Debt Restructuring, is approved and implemented. The Institute would allocate about $25 billion in newly issued SDRs to buy country debts in the secondary market, allowing debtor nations to internalize the discount.

The stock of debt could then be reduced under the condition that developing countries implement sound economic reforms.

Even assuming an agreement over longer maturities, substantial changes in the pricing structure, and more automatic refinancing of both amortization and interest, for some countries there may remain a need to reconcile long-term demand for external resources, from a steady growth prospective, with the private supply of funds in a non-market context.

Private banks may still provide residual new money on a case-by-case basis in order to assure the repayment of some interest. However, the increase in loan-loss reserves by large banks and the exit of the smaller regional ones suggest that new compulsory exposure will be restricted if it occurs at all. It will not, of course, allow positive new net inflows of private resources into debtor countries.

From this objective limitation on the actions of private banks, there arises the need for other long-term sources of funds, either from multilateral institutions (structural investments) or from government (trade-related). This complementary scheme should assure a sustainable level of current account deficit and a net positive inflow of external resources, or at least a nonnegative one, thus reversing the trend observed in recent years. A political decision will have to be made soon to increase the capital base of existing institutions and to expedite new channels for direct official resources. Otherwise it will be very difficult to escape from the pattern of adjustment with recession or low growth to a new stage of sustained growth.

Even if adjustment is reasonably successful, we cannot take it for granted that voluntary lending will resume automatically, not to a level compatible with the growth needs of LDCs. The recent crisis calls for a change in the nature of private banking in developing countries: banks are shifting from long-term project financing to trade-related operations. Long-term loans are becoming almost totally dependent on co-financing arrangements that transfer country risks to multilateral institutions.

In Chapter 4, I will return to other aspects of this proposal. Meanwhile, suffice it to stress that current rescheduling procedures need to be replaced by broad, innovative debt restructuring if we want to move toward a more permanent solution to the external debt issue.

Multiyear Rescheduling

The new approach contrasts sharply with the multiyear rescheduling that began with Mexico in 1984. On that occasion interest rates and new money were not included in the negotiations. I have tried to emphasize that these elements must be considered centerpieces in any long-term solution to the debt problem. This Mexican deal was limited to refinancing amortization coming due.[19] But this already had been taken for granted since the first timid rescheduling exercise. No bank could seriously expect to be paid back its principal amidst a liquidity crisis.

Implicit in the Mexican case is the idea that new money could be obtained normally, through the gradual restoration of voluntary lending. There is a basic contradiction here: if compulsory action is needed to assure the rollover of amortization not representing additional exposure for the banks, why should we expect spontaneous market action to supply new money, which necessarily represents an increase in exposure? In fact, what the banks actually hope for is to have the provision of long-term finance taken over by multilateral institutions with the help of co-financing schemes. The banks would then have the best of both worlds: zero increase in exposure to the debtor nations and full repayment of interest at market rates. But as we have seen, multilateral institutions do not yet have the capital to generate the flow of resources needed in an adjustment with growth context. Therefore, should this model be applied generally, the long-term possibilities for self-sustained growth for the developing countries would be reduced.

The need to revise Mexico's multiyear rescheduling by 1985 threw cold water on expectations of an early return to normal market conditions. The speed of Mexico's balance-of-payments swing from positive to negative following the fall in oil prices was blunt evidence of the vulnerability of debtor countries after many exercises in rescheduling. Tough negotiations followed, leading Mexico to the brink of a new default in order to assure a minimum inflow of new money, longer maturities, and reduced spreads. Some automatic compensation of additional external finance to offset lower oil prices and slow domestic growth was designed into the 1986 agreement. But it was not possible to achieve support for interest fluctuation or interest capitalization.

FIGURE 2.2   External Credit Squeeze – Net External Credits to
Indebted Developing Countries[a] *(US$ billion)*

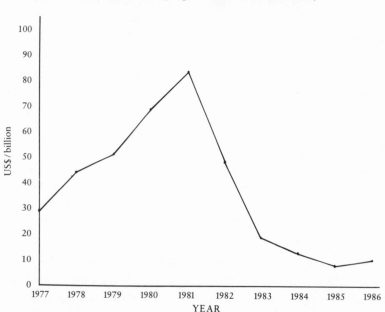

Source: World Bank
[a] Long and short term from private and official sources

This somewhat more flexible rescheduling was extended in 1987
to Argentina and the Philippines. Since signing a formal agreement with
the IMF is still a precondition under this form of rescheduling, it could
not have provided a means to avoid the Brazilian moratorium.

The Politics of Renegotiation

There is one final important issue, and it is strongly political: whether
it will take confrontation to bring about this new renegotiation strategy,
or whether consensus can be achieved more quietly. The matter is
speculative: on the plus side, despite the rigid posture adopted by banks
and governments of the major industrialized countries, the very evo-

lution of the crisis is forcing a revision in a more realistic direction. First, banks have raised their capital and reserves and are already writing off some of their assets and internalizing losses. Second, the overreaction of the banks has diminished their relative importance as a source of external finance. Third, the formal transformation of short-term credits (trade and interbank lines) into medium-term committed facilities has reduced the degree of vulnerability of some debtor countries; and finally, the LDC swing from capital importer to net capital exporter means that the question of repaying the debt has become more than ever a decision about the use of domestic resources. (Figure 2.2).

While the harshness of the times has gradually led to a convergence of objectives among debtor countries, among the banks there is now less cohesion than before. Rescheduling has diminished the differences in debt structure among Latin countries, and they are united by high U.S. interest rates. In contrast, banks are more divided than ever on how to deal with the impact of upredictable movements in external interest rates and the availability of new money. The need to increase their reserves and to account for losses is introducing sharp differences among major money center banks throughout the world: some are now in a stronger position; others with more limited ability to increase their reserves are becoming more vulnerable. Also, the open support given by the U.S. administration to Continental Illinois has further discouraged regional banks from taking part in additional loans to debtor countries. They feel the issue should be dealt with exclusively by the major banks, particularly now that the Federal Reserve will lend its support should trouble arise. (Table 2.4).

Greater reliance upon official resources will make the debt question more and more a political issue, whether the banks like it or not. The Latin countries finally have realized that coordinated action around common points is essential to force a change in the terms of reference. The Cartagena summit of May 1984 is a historic landmark in this direction. In future, ministers of foreign affairs probably will sit around renegotiation tables side-by-side with ministers of finance and central bank presidents. As the margins for technical adaptation in rescheduling exhaust themselves, it is not unlikely that politicians will take over command of the process.

World economic conditions will determine whether the next stage

TABLE 2.4   **Exposure of the International Banks** *(1983 in US$ billion)*

Selected Countries	Debt with Banks	Share of American Banks (%)
Mexico	69.8	38.2
Brazil	68.2	27.2
Venezuela	28.0	41.7
Argentina	27.1	34.5
Chile	11.8	49.7
Philippines	10.2	15.9
Yugoslavia	10.2	22.4

Source: The America Bank Review, "International Debt: Banks and the LDCs" Special Papers No. 10, London, March 1984.

of restructuring—probably along the general lines described here—will be reached through the consent of the key players or by unilateral action on the part of the debtors. Until now there has been a clear division on strategy among the three large Latin debtors: Brazil first suspended payments and is now beginning a complex and still undefined process of negotiation with private banks and possibly the IMF. Mexico and Argentina are following the more conventional road of rescheduling with the Fund.

If the expected slowdown in Western European economies over the next few years is not preceded by a substantial decline in the real U.S. interest rate (caused by stronger U.S. action on its domestic deficit), then the conditions will exist for radical action by Latin American countries. Simultaneous suspension of payment by Brazil, Mexico, and Argentina would be a serious threat to international finance. With the virtual disappearance of interregional Latin and African markets, newborn trade surpluses have been increasingly dependent on the behavior of developed economies, particularly the United States.[20] The performance of the American trade balance, where deficits are reaching historic levels despite the sharp devaluation of the dollar, will be crucial in coming chapters of the debt drama.

A solution for the Latin debt—to the extent that it rehabilitates the continent's ability to import—would facilitate the unavoidable but complex realignment of trade imbalances between the United States,

Europe, and Japan. The recent Japanese decision to recycle about $20 billion to the region is a first step in this direction.

The United States thus plays a vital role in the outcome of confrontation versus negotiation: either it will make a successful internal adjustment, drastically changing people's expectations about the domestic deficit and therefore about interest rates, or it will have to accept some unorthodox scheme to deal with the external debt question in order to prevent its own domestic finance system from collapsing.

3

Development vs. Adjustment: The Role of the IMF

The innovative role taken by the International Monetary Fund in putting pressure on commercial banks to reschedule LDC external debt runs counter to the way the Fund conducts the adjustment process within debtor countries. In putting pressure on banks, the IMF is recognizing the risk of waiting for the market to solve the credibility crisis following the Mexican default. It is adopting a consciously interventionist posture to prevent the collapse of international finance. By recognizing the unique nature of the current crisis — the virtual paralysis of markets — the IMF is discarding its historically neutral posture vis-à-vis private institutions. The IMF is taking up the baton to conduct a large and badly tuned orchestra.

In contrast, the IMF holds fast to conventional formulas for the management of aggregate demand within a country. The contrast between these approaches encourages short-term contingency policies to the detriment of more comprehensive economic reforms. In following these contradictory courses, the IMF unintentionally deepens the conflict between short-term and long-term objectives, particularly between adjustment and structural changes.

This contradiction reflects the IMF's origin at the Bretton Woods conference. In 1944 it made sense to distinguish between development and adjustment. The IMF was set up to tackle balance-of-payment issues, which were seen then as transitory. Development questions were to be dealt with by the World Bank, also conceived at Bretton Woods.

As the years have passed, and particularly after the first oil shock, it has been increasingly difficult to maintain the distinction between the problems of external adjustment and those of development. Disequilibrium in external accounts is no longer the result solely of commodity price fluctuations or distortions in the management of exchange policy: now it reflects more permanent changes in the energy price matrix and the relative prices of tradeables and nontradeables, which call for substantial changes in the production structure. Correction of external imbalances requires direct action on the supply of goods and services, particularly in the area of energy substitution, in addition to diversification of the export profile. No longer is it just a matter of skillful management of aggregate demand.

With the interest rate shock, the ensuing paralysis of financial markets, and the advent of external constraints, the interaction between adjustment and development becomes even more critical: the time spans needed to correct such imbalances are much longer than those assumed in formal IMF programs.

The changes the IMF has undertaken over the past few years are minor in view of the profound alterations in the nature of economic problems. Important amendments to its by-laws were made in 1969, with the introduction of special drawing rights (SDRs) and in 1978, to recognize the abandonment of the fixed exchange rate system since the beginning of the 1970s.[1] Another major change was the introduction of the EFF in 1974, which lengthened the adjustment period from the one-year deadline prevailing in standby agreements to three years. Most debtor countries are now under this three-year program. During the critical years of the debt crisis, such an agreement would provide a country with access to resources equivalent to 450 percent of its quota. In the case of Brazil, this equalled a total loan volume of $4.6 billion, disbursed on the three-year schedule.

Resources available from the IMF have become increasingly modest in the face of the magnitude of disequilibrium to be managed. In the two-year period, 1982–1983, IMF resources made up 20 percent of the net external finance to non-oil-producing LDCs. Direct IMF resources to Brazil in the 1982–1984 adjustment program amounted to $4.5 billion—again, 20 percent of the total net inflow of financial resources.

The IMF has undergone a lengthy process of capital impairment more visible when compared with the expansion of international trade: its quotas have gone from 16 percent of the overall trade value in 1945 to about 3 percent in 1984. Paradoxically, as external imbalances mount, the potential for direct contribution by the IMF shrinks, which helps explain why the Fund has come to work directly with international banks: given the limitations on its internal resources, this association is critical to assure that current account deficits remain sustainable. The new relationship between the IMF and the banks has political as well as economic implications.

Intervention by the IMF has not prevented extremely low external levels from occurring. Replenishment of reserves is slow and entirely dependent on the trade balance. In Brazil, despite remarkable performance in the trade balance, within two years of IMF intervention net reserves immediately available had reached only $3 billion.[2] This figure is short of the safety level, given world economic uncertainties and changes in the domestic economy, as the events following the so-called Cruzado plan in 1986 have shown. Even with the modest resources available from the IMF, disbursements are made over time and are tied strictly to compliance with present economic targets. In this framework, an increase in reserves is a sort of reward for those who have managed to get good grades in implementing their adjustment programs.

If it is to interrupt an unfavorable cycle of market behavior, IMF intervention should be designed to ensure a minimum volume of reserves, even *before* the actual cut of external deficits. By reducing uncertainty, such exogenously generated liquidity improves expectations and should make external adjustment faster and more effective.

Given the Polish and Mexican defaults, banks have concluded that there is no guarantee for a sovereign loan except a country's willingness to honor its commitments. The IMF is seen as a means to translate national expressions of goodwill or hope into a formal commitment. It has emerged as a guarantor for debtor countries to the commercial banks. In this new alliance between private banks and the IMF, the latter participates indirectly in determining the financial resources the banks will supply. A rigid and formal connection is introduced between implementation of the adjustment program, including internally related matters, and access to external finance. Existence of an agreement with the IMF becomes a requirement for any rescheduling that includes new credits, including government borrowing within the framework of the Club of Paris.[3]

The relationship among the IMF member countries and commercial banks is increasingly complex. The IMF's power to intervene in the decisions of private institutions about the level of resources they will allocate is limited. This is a job for monetary authorities. The Fund tries to prevent an even more drastic liquidity squeeze. But informal IMF action has not been enough to change the essence of the banks' decisionmaking policy, still geared to the prompt reduction of exposure in debtor countries.

Adverse Impact on World Trade

The IMF takes no direct part in negotiations between countries and banks. Nor does it intervene in setting loan costs — interest rates, spreads, or fees. So, unwittingly, the IMF supports a skewed adjustment process, whereby each country's current account deficit must adjust unilaterally to given conditions of external liquidity. This decentralized format of negotiations aggravates conflicting objectives among the parties. It is akin to trying to solve a system of simultaneous equations by solving each one independently. This is especially true from the viewpoint of the world economy, which requires that the interrelationship between the adjustment of each country and its impact on international trade be considered together.

By avoiding wholehearted involvement in rescheduling negotiations, where it could take on a very useful conciliatory role, the IMF has failed to bring about the participant's commitment to a program that will do what is needed: reduce external disequilibrium while allocating adequate financing. Unless both of these occur, external adjustment will not be efficient or sustainable. The sharp decline of imports in the period 1982–1986 reflects this distortion. In Latin America alone, import reduction over that period amounted to $44.6 billion and contributed directly to the slowdown in economic activity. Unemployment and the curtailment of economic growth entailed by the contraction of international trade are economic and social costs that must be taken into account in assessing the present adjustment process.

Another feature of the IMF program, the method by which it sets performance targets for debtor nations seeking its help, has further aggravated the decline in imports. Targets set for the current account deficit and maximum level of external indebtedness (the logical counterpart of ensured volume of financing) are commitments that can be achieved in the short run only by curbing imports. An important clause prevents a country from placing any restrictions on international payments beyond those that were in force at the time agreement was reached with the IMF. Whatever the behavior of exports, the country may not stop payment of interest, dividends, and royalties; nor is it permitted to accumulate trade arrears. Any deviation in external accounts must be offset entirely through new import cuts. This policy is particularly unfair where deviations in the balance of payments are caused by U.S. interest rate fluctuations rather than by any matter over which the country has control.

The IMF has not brought pressure on the parties to include price (interest) as well as quantity (volume of financing) as subjects for the negotiation table; instead, it has become an instrument for the protection of the international financial market by assuring a regular flow of interest payments at market rates.

There is a clear asymmetry between the adjustment of service and capital accounts on the one hand and adjustment of the trade account on the other. Unstable external interest rates and complex imbalances within the debtor countries have led the IMF—albeit involuntarily— to induce the contraction of international trade. Simultaneous cuts of imports by several Latin American countries have resulted in the virtual extinction of intraregional trade, which represented a growing share of Brazilian exports of manufactured goods. It is difficult to reconcile such an outcome with Article I, paragraph 2 of the IMF by-laws, which states the Fund's basic purpose as "facilitating a balanced expansion and growth of international trade." In short, the IMF has neither the resources nor the mechanisms to facilitate external adjustment without harming trade flows. In admission of this contradiction between its practices and the Articles of Agreement, the IMF has tried to force more liberal trade policies on some countries — Mexico and Argentina, for example. It has not, however, succeeded in altering the conditions of supplying external resources, nor has it changed the many forms of protectionism practiced by developed countries.

Interference in Domestic Economies

Recent multiyear agreements have transformed the IMF into a special and permanent auditor of debtor countries on behalf of the world financial system.[4] Ideally, once a mutually agreed upon adjustment program has been completed, the IMF should return to its regular follow-up system. Then the evaluation of a given country's performance would be confidential and would bear no relation to private banks. But under these new agreements, a multiyear IMF has emerged, extending for years the current strict automatic relationship between country performance and access to external financing.

It is hard to find support for the IMF's new supervisory role in by-laws that historically have been read to oppose differential treatment among member countries. In fact, this was a point of heated discussion when the IMF was born: LDCs, and India in particular, advocated differential treatment among countries as a function of their stage of development. At the time, the position of the developed countries prevailed. Now differentiation is being attempted by the IMF, in a clear step backward. Within the system that has been taking shape since the Mexican rescheduling, countries will come under special surveillance by the Fund even though they may have no access either to IMF resources or to new money from the banks.

This new IMF role is politically unacceptable to LDCs and makes little sense economically. Conditionalities can be seen by debtor countries as the price they pay for access to resources not available otherwise. But where the IMF has no new finance to offer, it is not appropriate for it to insist on continuing intervention. All these important issues stress the need for a review of the IMF's procedures for internal adjustment and a profound change in methods of defining the supply of external resources. Such a step would represent an important, positive change of attitude. At present, no one—neither banks nor governments—wants to commit additional resources toward meeting the growth needs of debtor nations; yet everyone's criteria for internal adjustment remain rigid and unrealistic.

When a loan is made at terms more favorable than the market, a borrower properly expects added conditions to be placed on it. When credit is provided for regional, industrial, or agricultural development programs at better-than-market rates and maturities, a set of obligations commonly is accepted by the borrower to measure project implementation against pre-set targets. The existence of some conditionalities for IMF-backed financing is fair and proper: the IMF is simply trying to assure repayment of loans, thereby acting as institutional collateral in the place of real guarantees, by definition nonexistent. Conditionalities put in place ostensibly to ensure correction of the source of disequilibrium in external accounts help to lay the groundwork for countries to honor their financial commitments.

The system employed by the IMF goes beyond what is proper to ensure repayment of loans, however. It explicitly includes economic policy targets and goals for the correction of *internal* imbalances. It is in the relationship between external and internal adjustments where the Fund's stabilization programs confront a mine field of political sensitivities.

IMF Inflexibility

The theory dealing simultaneously with external and internal adjustments is based—as Professor Simonsen has shown—on the monetarist concept of a balance of payments in a framework of fixed exchange rates.[5] In such a framework there is a direct correlation between expansion of the domestic money supply—mostly through financing the public deficit—and deterioration of the external accounts through

the accumulation of trade balance deficits. Excessive expansion creates too much aggregate demand, affecting the external sector by
increasing a country's imports and reducing the availability of its goods
for export. External competitiveness is limited by the simultaneous
increase in domestic inflation and exchange rigidity. The unavoidable
result is a disequilibrium in the trade balance. Under this scheme the
public deficit is reflected as a deficit in the balance of payments. Sustained external adjustment therefore calls for the correction of internal imbalances, particularly control over the expansion of domestic
credit.

The theory has several limitations. First, external disequilibrium
is seen as internally caused. The theory does not concern itself with
imbalances caused by factors not related to domestic policy. Second,
the theory is based on a short-term model, and discards matters connected with capital accumulation and growth. Last, we now live in a
world of flexible exchange rates where there is no longer an automatic
relationship between variations of international reserves and monetary aggregates.

This elegant but incomplete theoretical framework is the basis
for IMF programs. It provides the rationale for selecting variables to
measure program implementation, so-called performance criteria, both
external (current account deficit and indebtedness) and internal (domestic credit, public financing). Quantitative limits are set for these variables and must be adhered to strictly over a short period of time, usually
one quarter. Noncompliance with targets automatically leads to an
interruption of IMF disbursements. Since there is now in practice a
direct and formal connection between access to Fund resources and
access to credit from banks, any deviation in program implementation,
even if internal, may halt completely the flow of external finance. For
debtor LDCs this is one of the worst features of IMF enforcement. It
must be reassessed in view of the variable nature of the disequilibrium
in question.

In addition to quantitative goals, the IMF also sets *qualitative* targets. For each of its now vast numbers of involuntary clientele, it calls
for adjustment of the exchange rate, subsidy cuts, price deregulation,
and elimination of negative real interest rates. Such commonality of
treatment may reflect a remarkable similarity among the problems of

countries, or it may show that the IMF sticks close to its theory. The internal problems of developing countries do share some common points. But to invoke a standard treatment requires concentration on just a handful of junctural issues. This is a major limitation of IMF programs — their excessive focus on short-term policies related to the management of aggregate demand, relegating critical supply-side issues to minor status.

If the IMF's theoretical backgrounds favor the uniform application of a limited set of junctural rather than structural variables, so does the need to select easily measured indicators. The IMF budgetary constraints limit what it can do — particularly in its programs. With its continuous depletion of capital the IMF finds it increasingly difficult to make adjustment periods flexible, and it finds that rigid conditionalities are needed as a means to ration the demand for its resources.

Whether the reason is the theoretical assumptions held by the IMF or its practical problems, its present methods are not effective. Application of a minimum adjustment period across the board fails to recognize acute structural and institutional differences among debtor countries. The time span for such an adjustment program should be negotiated, not given. Likewise, it makes no sense to use a single time schedule to evaluate the entire set of variables within the system of conditionalities.

Although internal adjustment should be dovetailed with external adjustment, the IMF ties them together rigidly quarter by quarter, for no good reason. The result is the "quarterly syndrome," whereby any program deviation may automatically trigger an external liquidity squeeze.

Measuring Failure, or a Failure of Measures

The two-year results (1983–1984) of a formal adjustment program in Brazil were not good: inflation was consistently higher than original projections; the public deficit at the end of 1984 was greater than it had been at the start of the program; the economy remained vulnerable to changing external conditions; and, most important, it was impossible to achieve adjustment with self-sustained growth.[6] There are, of

course, macroeconomic reasons behind such a failure, not just institutional problems aggravated by the IMF. These are examined in the next
chapter. For now let us see how the adjustment methodology utilized
by the IMF has contributed to these difficulties.

Even the EFF, which is considered a structural adjustment, has
relatively limited scope and severely underestimates the time required
for implementation of institutional reforms directed at the sources of
disequilibria. The IMF has been too much too soon. Basically, every
country that took advantage of the EFF has been forced to ask for waiv-
ers because problems — some social, some political — have prevented
them from reaching their original targets.[7] These troubles reflect,
among other things, unrealistic goals that were set to meet a tight adjustment schedule. This pre-fixed time for stabilization leads to drastic
underestimation of the lag between the adoption of reforms and their
effect upon the economy.

Since it works with nominal variables and quarterly targets, the
IMF is forced to forecast the behavior of the inflation rate a year in
advance. Although it is not declared as such, monthly inflation becomes
a key variable in evaluating economic performance. Chronic inflation,
such as that prevailing in Latin America, is characterized not only by
price increases but also by large variations from month to month in
the rate of increase. These rates cannot be predicted accurately. Substantial deviation between price increase targets and actual inflation
is common. Brazil's second letter of intention signed in September 1983,
forecast a 5 percent monthly inflation rate for the last quarter of the
year. Actual rates were around 10 percent. The predicted monthly rate
for the last quarter of 1984 was 2.5 percent. It actually came to four
times that level. An addendum to the September 1983 letter, drafted
in March 1984, forecast that inflation would fall by half throughout
the year. Actual figures indicate a higher inflation rate in 1984 (224
percent) than recorded in 1983 (211 percent).

If these deviations meant nothing more than embarrassment for
failing to meet targets — something like a statistical neurosis — they might
be tolerated, although this would no doubt affect the credibility of the
program, which in itself would make it more difficult to enforce anti-
inflation policy. But the main problem is the impact on quarterly limits variables that make up the evaluation system. Any gap between the

projected and actual inflation rate requires an automatic and almost instantaneous offsetting adjustment. Sensitivity of the program to inflation rates is especially acute in the Brazilian case because of our compulsory generalized indexation. It quickly spreads any exogenous price shock throughout the economic system.[8]

Measuring the Public Deficit

The IMF attempts to measure the public deficit on the basis of financial flows, i.e., by the variation in total indebtedness of the public sector, both internal and external. This is the famous PSB (Public Sector Borrowing) index designed to evaluate the behavior of the deficit in nominal terms and thus to incorporate fluctuations in financing costs. The PSB index is of the utmost importance in gauging the extent to which the private sector is crowded out of access to funds by the upward pressure of public sector borrowing on interest rates. The PSB is also useful for measuring the relationship between public deficit and inflation as they are affected indirectly through the formation of expectations.

The PSB is not, however, the relevant measure to use in assessing the *sources* of internal disequilibrium, in other words, for evaluating the structural makeup of the public deficit. Through this indicator we see the consequences of disequilibrium in the public accounts; it does not give us a view of what is *behind* the imbalances. For this, another measure is required—the operational deficit—that should reflect as closely as possible the real disequilibrium.

Only through the use of two such complementary indicators— financial needs and operational imbalances—can a consistent analysis of the evolution of public deficit be achieved. The operating or structural measure completes the framework to forecast inflation, especially on a long-term basis: it is an approximate measure of *the potential* public deficit, vital to economic agent's expectations about trends in prices. The *nominal* deficit has a stronger effect on short-term expectations.

Perhaps the best example of the IMF's dogmatic approach and its excessive concern about short-term problems is its application of the PSB method in the Brazilian case. Annual targets were frustrated repeatedly by unpredictable inflation rates. The initial target was to reduce PSB from 14 percent of GDP in 1982, to 7.9 percent in 1983; in the September 15, 1983 letter of intent, the target was reset to 15.4 percent; and on November 14 of the same year a revision was made to 18.6 percent of GDP as a function of the substantial gap between projected and actual inflation. The December 1984 letter of intent admitted that even the latter figure probably would fall short. Wide fluctuation in one of the critical parameters for evaluation of the economic program raises the suspicion that it might not be suitable as an indicator of adjustment progress. Successive changes bring doubts about the consistency of the stabilization program itself.

Difficulties also were encountered in pre-setting quarterly limits for the nominal deficit. Differences between forecast and actual indexation are the counterpart of deviation in the trajectory of inflation, and severely affect service of the public debt. Any attempt to offset these differences in the short run through new expense cuts or even increased taxation come up against practical and legal limitations. In these circumstances the problem is not a lack of political will to curb the deficit, but rather the impossibility of doing so under the conditions set by IMF policies.

Several distortions are generated by the IMF's rigid posture. Tax increases are often resorted to for their prompt enforcement and resulting revenue, taking no account of their allocative effects. In Brazil, a classical example is the intensive use that was made of the tax rate for financial operations (IOF) that changed several times in a single year without the need for congressional approval. Another example is the withholding tax on financial assets, set at such a high level that it discourages voluntary savings and leads to an increase in interest rates.

The use of a financial indicator to measure the evolution of public deficit may direct all efforts to the pure and simple curtailment of loans to the public sector without getting to the root of the problem. The result is often just a freeze on the deficit rather than a true reduction. Taken to extremes, it may limit access to credit by public sector borrowers who require working capital to increase operating income in order to reduce their own deficits.

Inflationary expectations are usually based on an assessment of continuous efforts to cut the deficit rather than on episodic measures.

The use of a time span as short as a quarter to measure the evolution of public deficit nearly always leads to revenue advances or to the artificial containment of expenses to meet performance criteria, which does nothing to reduce the public imbalances.

Difficulties encountered in strict application of the short-term public deficit criterion to Brazil, particularly following the 1983 maxi devaluation, became so evident that in July of that year the IMF agreed to include operational measures in the letters of intent along with the nominal deficit. But the change was excessively timid. The new parameter was not granted the status of a performance criterion but was treated as just another economic indicator. The IMF should have reversed the roles and made a comprehensive and accurate indicator of the operational deficit the major criterion, and applied it to a longer time span, at least six months. Deviation in the nominal deficit occurring simultaneously with decline in the operational deficit, as now defined, would reflect only genuine errors in inflation targets when nominal ceilings were established. They would more accurately reflect the complexity of the lags that follow an inflationary trend, and there would be no need for gimmicks such as the temporary containment of overall financing.

Systematic growth of both the nominal deficit conventionally measured by the IMF, and the operational deficit would mean that no progress was being made toward adjustment of the public sector. Both indicators must be used simultaneously to allow for a consistent analysis of events. The operational deficit used here should be broadly re-evaluated, with its components disaggregated as far as possible. That would be the only way to pinpoint the sources of disequilibrium and to establish an appropriate counterstrategy.

The approach I am proposing is distinct from the current definition of operational deficit: excessive aggregation and the way it is estimated necessarily lead to underestimation of the extent of the disequilibrium. The IMF referred to a "modest operating surplus" for late 1984. The revised numbers pointed to a deficit of 2–3 percent of GDP.

In more recent years, both operational and financial deficits have been growing, and they are feeding a sharp acceleration of inflation, only temporarily and artificially reduced through price and wage freezes in 1986, and again in the second semester of 1987.

Compensatory Monetary Policy

In principle, monetary policy may be employed, even over a short period to offset deviations in the adjustment program. IMF methods often induce a combination of short-term policies in LDCs that end up placing too much emphasis on monetary instruments and increase dependence of the adjustment process on the behavior of the interest rate. In 1984 Brazil attempted to limit expansion of the monetary base to 50 percent in order to offset the congressional defeat of a government bill proposing a reduction in wage indexation. The target was soon perceived to be unrealistic and had to be revised upward to 100 percent at mid-year reflecting limitations to the implementation of a monetary squeeze. Frequent revisions of targets and instruments negatively affect the reliability of a stabilization program, raising serious doubts about its consistency.

Methodological difficulties also were present in selecting the appropriate monetary aggregate. Based on the previously mentioned theoretical model, the IMF at first selected net domestic credit as a performance criterion. But in Brazil this variable was quite sensitive to fluctuations in so-called foreign currency deposits at the Central Bank, whose short-run behavior is largely outside the control of monetary authorities.[9] After July 1983, the impact of this external component was excluded from the calculations of net domestic credit, and the more conventional concept of monetary base was again taken up.

A development that occurred in 1984 illustrates what is likely to happen when predetermined evaluation systems are implemented rigidly: Brazil formally met its net domestic credit targets, but the monetary base shot up to record levels of around 248 percent, contributing to worsening inflation.

In developing countries there are objective limits to the extent that monetary policy can be tightened unilaterally. Because public sector demand for funds is inelastic, the usual result of tightening the money supply is to push real interest rates too high with a disproportionate negative impact on the private sector. The vulnerability of the financial sector, which is often undercapitalized, is increased by the rapid deterioration of assets. These two factors combine to limit the extent and intensity of a monetary squeeze.

A coherent monetary policy can be implemented only where basic sources of public sector imbalance are eliminated. The degree of substitution possible between fiscal and monetary policy in such economies is limited. This fundamental issue needs to be recognized in setting up the concrete timetable of policy measures in stabilization programs.

IMF policy could lead to a sequence of events such as the following: 1) Formal time restrictions for enforcement of the adjustment program demand setting unrealistic targets for cutting back inflation. 2) These targets are incorporated into quarterly performance criteria. 3) Despite implementation of the agreed-upon measures, and therefore compliance with qualitative criteria, a short-run differential arises between observed inflation and projected inflation. 4) As a result, an internal target, say the level of public deficit, is not achieved. 5) Noncompliance leads to interruption of IMF disbursements and automatically of credit from commercial banks. Given such a course of events, an external liquidity crisis is triggered no matter what might be happening to the balance of payment. The true cause was a short-term deviation in internal adjustment, the origin of which was an evaluation error in estimating the behavior of inflation.

Something similar to this scenario actually occurred in Brazil when inflation was grossly underestimated because of the February 1982 maxi-devaluation. Inability to meet public deficit targets necessitated revising the program and requesting a waiver from the IMF. Five months were required to renegotiate nominal ceilings, and another ten to redesign the external financing arrangement. Meanwhile, precisely when performance of the Brazilian trade balance was improving, an acute liquidity crisis occurred, and arrears accumulated because the country could not disburse the bank's credit nor the IMF's own resources.

At year-end 1983, newly accelerated inflation added to the difficulty of complying with the pre-set nominal ceilings. An unusual open-market operation was required, whereby short-term federal treasury bonds (LTNs)—precisely the best security for implementing monetary policy in the framework of unpredictable inflation—were massively replaced by exchange-indexed securities (ORTNs), for the simple reason that interest costs could be spread over time.[10] (Under the discount system used with LTNs, financial costs are allocated when the security is placed in the market.) This is a striking example of how the rigid methodology of the IMF can lead to distortions in the implementation of short-run policies. Brazil is not alone in this dilemma. Similar problems have occurred in Argentina, Chile, and Mexico, to mention only the most glaring examples.

The New System of Conditionalities

The question, therefore, is not the existence of conditionalities but their nature and how they are to be applied. The crucial issue is to reconcile the acknowledged structural diagnosis of the crisis with the IMF's patterns of action. The need to make the adjustment period more flexible has already been mentioned as a means to relieve the pressure of overly ambitious targets. We know little about the lags between measures and results of economic policy, particularly in the fight against inflation. For an effective structural adjustment program, the primary emphasis should be on *qualitative* aspects of the required changes. The program should be judged on the consistency of measures adopted rather than on their short-term quantitative impacts, which can only be discovered after the fact. Trying to predict these variations accurately is an exercise in frustration. If the measures are consistent, positive results will come about sooner or later, but it is impossible to estimate when.

Nominal ceilings should be as realistic as possible. Additional compensatory measures should be applied only when deviation from targets give a true indication that agreed-upon policies have not been implemented. Differences in response to price lags, whose precise distribution over time is never accurately known, should be acknowledged as inherent in the dynamics of inflation. Should complementary compensation be unavoidable in, say, the fiscal area, it would not be implemented on a case-by-case basis just to meet the formality of a quarterly limit. Not only would legal restrictions be taken into account, but also allocative implications and long-term impacts. For this purpose, a new agreement about the nature of the measures would suffice for the program to be set in motion again.

In the broader adjustment framework discussed here, it is essential to introduce explicitly a set of structural variables in the system of conditionalities side-by-side with the conventional short-term variables utilized by the IMF. Such variables would establish a logical connection between necessary demand management policies and long-term measures. The adjustment process would become more efficient and have a greater chance of being sustained over time. Correction of disequilibrium would be permanent.

Private investment, import levels, and social indicators are examples of structural conditionalities that should undergo revision only once a year. Setting a bottom line for private investment would prevent the cut in public deficit from being carried out exclusively through higher taxes or an excessive requirement for private saving. Likewise, *a priori* setting of a minimum import ceiling would prevent a fall in the current account deficit "at any cost," i.e., by treating imports as residuals. Such conditionalities would require additional external financing, now overly contracted, and would force the IMF into a more active role in determining liquidity levels. Finally, defining social indicators would allow us to carry on critical government spending — in health and education for example — and avoid indiscriminate slashing of public expenditures. It is impossible to ignore the social issue in developing countries, even when the economy must submit to severe constraints.

For logical and practical reasons, the current automatic pegging of internal adjustment to external liquidity should be discarded. It makes no sense to squeeze any country into a quarterly time frame. Negotiated external resources should constitute a firm commitment over a minimum period of time, say one year. This is particularly true where there is an asymmetrical relationship between external and internal performance. According to current IMF methodology, access to external resources may be interrupted because of deviation in the internal parameters despite any significant accumulation of trade surpluses.

It is reasonable to maintain that continuous deviation from scheduled targets and lack of compensatory action justify suspension of disbursements. Otherwise the system of conditionalities makes no sense. What is being questioned is the automatic link established over the very short run between internal performance and external liquidity. This is an extremely important point, as there is a formal connection between IMF resources and access to bank credit.

Still on the institutional level, more coordination is needed between the two sister institutions, the IMF and the World Bank. Such coordination would be the logical outcome of recognizing the infeasibility of distinguishing between adjustment and development in the present scenario. Furthermore, credits from multilateral organizations would carry greater weight in the supply of long-term resources to developing countries. World Bank action might be decisive in assuring continuity of investment directed to export diversification and energy substitution.

Despite official rhetorics and physical proximity (the institutions are next door to each other in Washington and are connected by a long hallway), in practice the coordination between them is minor. There is no World Bank representative at negotiations with the IMF. An example of the inconsistency that results from this lack of coordination is that funds allocated by the World Bank to Brazil's alcohol program could not be used effectively because of limitations that were imposed by the IMF on the expansion of internal credit.

IMF Future

The foregoing analysis suggests that a reformulation of the system of conditionalities would in no way detract from the stimulus needed to implement the adjustment, but rather would render the process more effective and therefore lay the groundwork for its continuity. The current methodology boosts uncertainties unnecessarily and forces concentration of effort almost exclusively on short-term policies while neglecting their medium- and long-term implications. Targets are set, not for consistency with the instruments adopted, but to satisfy program formalities, especially the timeframe, leading to frequent revisions that undermine credibility.

On the external side, the limited IMF resources and poorly defined maneuvering room with private banks has resulted in a model of "adjustment without liquidity," thus placing a disproportionate share of the burden for reduction of disequilibrium on a nation's trade account relative to its service and capital accounts. For the IMF, an institution whose basic objective is to create conditions for the balanced growth of international trade, the spin-offs of the Mexican shock—particularly the drastic cutback of imports in debtor countries—have been frustrating. These events have demonstrated how modest the IMF's margin is for effective countercyclical action.

Broader redefinition of the IMF's role requires a new political posture among industrialized countries. The IMF's actions reflect the viewpoints of member countries, among them the small group of industrialized countries that hold *de facto* political power within the organization—the twenty-one countries that have 58 percent of the votes. Developing countries, despite their growing numbers (the People's Republic of China and Hungary were recently added) and the trend toward an increase in their relative share of world trade, have not managed to expand their voting power. Some IMF initiatives, such as creation of the Development Committee and the EFF, are timid attempts to accommodate pressure exerted by these countries. Only the Arab countries, through Saudi Arabia, have been able to nominate their own executive director in recognition of the financial support they provide the institution.

The posture adopted by the governments of industrialized countries has been to support the principle of minimum external intervention and maximum internal adjustment. The conservative side, represented by the current American, British, and German governments, has systematically opposed efforts to correct undercapitalization of the IMF or to allow a reassessment of the system of conditionalities. Recent quota increases have been modest in view of world needs, so much so that EFF programs have been forced to reduce IMF credits from 450 percent of quotas to a maximum of 150 percent. Tightening of conditionalities is another means of rationing IMF resources.

The IMF's power structure makes it impossible to apply the principle of uniform treatment to member countries. The IMF is powerless, for instance, to intervene in the ill-combined American monetary and fiscal policies, today the factor chiefly responsible for high interest rates. Symmetric surveillance and forceful action to end sources of imbalances among different countries were never implemented.

The debt crisis has demonstrated the need for institutional mechanisms to compensate for market imbalances. Intervention is essential to help the reconstruction of a private financial market for debtor countries. *It is crucial that the IMF be reinforced with new resources, and its mechanisms and action guidelines be revamped.* That is a precondition for the achievement of basic objectives, still valid today—especially external equilibrium and the expansion of economic activity—but being sought in a different world from that of Bretton Woods.

Greater availability of resources and more operational flexibility are the only means to create sound conditions in place of the current system in which access to IMF programs can be gained only on a compulsory basis after all other liquidity sources have been exhausted. Conditions must be created to encourage the more rational alternative of going to the IMF voluntarily in anticipation of future difficulties, and therefore with minimum loss of external liquidity. Present reluctance to go to the IMF often reflects the limited availability of resources when assessed against its rigid system of conditionalities. Countries fear that credit provided by the IMF will not be enough to offset the suspension of international bank credit that normally takes place until negotiation of the adjustment program is complete. The IMF needs more liquidity just to facilitate orderly access to its stabilization programs.

If the IMF's capital base kept up with the expansion of international trade, theoretically Brazil would have access to roughly $18 billion under the extended fund facility, in contrast to the $4.6 billion effectively disbursed.[11] That would change the entire current format of external adjustment, and might lay the foundation for longer-term and therefore more realistic internal adjustment programs. Should the current trend continue, the IMF's influence will decline. Its resources are not sufficient to alter substantially the state of external liquidity. Nor does the IMF have the legal power or the support of industrialized countries necessary to influence bank decisionmaking.

Under current conditions, therefore, the net benefit from an association with the IMF falls sharply once the peak of a liquidity crisis is over. Unilateral attempts by the banks to design a new IMF role tied to multiyear rescheduling, without any substantial additional commitment of resources, made little sense to the developing countries. Lack of political leadership and initiative from the industrialized nations leaves the IMF short of the means to act equitably and effectively should there be a new wave of financial shocks.

It should be recognized, however, that some new features were introduced in the recent Mexican and Argentinian stabilization programs, making performance criteria more flexible. But given the magnitude of the present debt crisis, these steps are only a timid attempt.

4

Internal Equilibrium and the Issue of External Debt

The Brazilian debt crisis of the 1980s should be understood as the end of an era. It is more than a junctural or cyclical crisis and it is more than a liquidity crunch. The observable financial disequilibrium, external and internal, is only the tip of the iceberg, the visible manifestation of a profoundly unbalanced structure underneath.

To put the country back on the path to growth, new institutional arrangements are needed. The intensity of both external and internal changes has made the current framework for economic policy obsolete. Its modernization is essential. The institutional reforms required are more than technical. They will demand skill and courage to mobilize broad political support, not only to deal with internal issues but for external problems as well. The coincidence of the economic crisis with Brazil's political transition should be explored in a positive sense. Political liberalization is essential for the emergence of new leadership that can bring about the necessary level of public support for needed changes in the domestic economy.

The End of an Era

During the past twenty years, Brazil, like many developing countries and like most of Latin America, has pursued a development strategy aimed at rapid growth financed by external resources and led by direct and indirect state intervention. Early in this period, subsidies and price control were introduced. Over the years the state gradually enlarged its scope of direct intervention by mobilizing domestic savings and moving to the forefront of investment activity in a variety of key sectors. Through its unique ability to unite economic resources and political power, the state has expanded its activity from correcting market distortions to broad intervention, and it has become the main internal source of disequilibrium. For a brief, bright period, central economic planning was seen almost as a *deus ex machina*, the unlimited wisdom of which contrasted sharply with the working difficulties of market forces. But not for long. Economic planning soon became the vehicle for massive growth of the public sector.

Domestically, the government uses its monopoly power to finance expansion of the public sector through the inflation tax.[1] External growth with indebtedness would not have been possible without the state acting in its new role as sovereign borrower in the world financial market. Somehow, when the state did the borrowing, the risk to the lender disappeared from sight. In fact, the label "sovereign borrower" was coined to enable international banks to believe in magic: no risk and high returns. Until the Polish and Mexican shocks, no one in the international financial market really thought a country would default, forgetting as they did the many important examples from the past.

Two factors in particular have helped extend the life of this pattern of unbalanced growth, one internal and the other external. Internally, indexation has left some room for voluntary savings, and thereby shrank the base upon which inflationary taxes are charged. In a highly indexed system, the only way to assure the transfer of real resources through inflation taxes is through the continuous acceleration of inflation. This helps explain the escalation of inflation levels since 1973 following growth in the public deficit. Externally, as we have seen, domestic restrictions on the financial system led to the rapid internationalization of private banks and the development of an international dollar-based money market. Accumulation of monetary surpluses by a handful of oil-producing countries provided major resources for this new market framework.

The rapid growth of deposits made the supply of external resources highly elastic, and rendered access to the international financial market nearly automatic. Competition to lend money to LDC sovereign borrowers was brisk. Plentiful liquidity prevailed until 1978, predominately at *negative* real interest rates. Add to this the absence of qualitative limitations (conditionalities), and it becomes clear that resorting heavily to external indebtedness was irresistible for most LDCs.

Maintaining State Interventionism, Postponing Adjustment

The combination of supply-side competition to make loans and demand-side concentration in the hands of the state set the basis for explosive indebtedness and led to the 1982 crisis. The odd association between private competition and state monopoly helps explain how Brazil and other developing countries were able to delay for so long responsible adjustment to the exogenous shocks of the previous decade. In reaction to the fourfold increase in the price of oil in 1973–1974, we financed the external disequilibrium by gradual reduction of the current account deficit, in the hope that the shock would be transitory. When increased energy costs led to worldwide recession, Brazil's government was able to act countercyclically, expanding public investment and stimulating private investment. This strategy kept our growth rate above its natural trend (though still below the 1968–1973 levels), at the expense of nearly doubled inflation and greatly increased external and internal indebtedness. The presence of the state in the economy and easy international credit made the decision to put off adjustment possible.

Then, in 1978–1979, the world was hit by both a new oil shock and a sudden shift from negative real interest rates to high positive ones. Suddenly there was a big jump in the cost of both oil and interest payments. Again the government postponed adjustment, sustaining economic growth by printing money (inflation reached 100 per cent per year) and borrowing abroad.

The institutional rigidity of the Brazilian economy is a direct result of public sector expansion: excessive state intervention, indebtedness, and inflation are links in the chain with which we have shackled ourselves. External factors beyond our control, such as oil prices and interest rates, are fairly blamed for much of our debt problem. But excessive state expansion is also a big part of the problem, and it is our own doing. This is true of all three major Latin American debtors, Brazil, Argentina, and Mexico. It largely explains the relative economic health of Colombia, where the level of state intervention is smaller. And at the other end of the scale, it helps explain why the crisis also has hit socialist countries, particularly those with centrally planned economies—Poland, especially, and Hungary less severely. It shows why Southeast Asia's developing countries—Korea and Taiwan—have weathered the storm more smoothly. The explanation lies in their institutional flexibility, particularly with respect to the allocation of resources between tradeables and nontradeables.

The three major Latin American debtors underwent sharp and unbalanced public sector growth: in the 1970–1982 period, overall public sector expenditures as a percentage of GDP increased from 33 per cent to 35 per cent in Argentina, from 28 per cent to 32 per cent in Brazil, and from 21 per cent to 48 per cent in Mexico. More impressive is the rapid accumulation of disequilibrium. In the early 1970s these countries presented slight deficits, 1 to 2 per cent of GDP, easily financed without causing inflation. By contrast, in the years leading to the debt crisis, public deficits surged to 14 to 17 per cent and became a major factor in the acceleration of prices.[2] Such was the domestic counterpart of postponing unavoidable adjustment.

The magnitude of external disequilibrium and the acceleration of inflation in 1978–1979 deeply affected business expectations in Brazil and quickly led to a substantial reduction in private investment. The characteristic inertia of the public sector, on the other hand, meant that curtailment of public spending was slower. In fact, the need to ensure a minimum volume of external financing made it difficult suddenly to cut back public sector imports because of the interrelationship between long-term financing and supplier's credit. The public deficit issue was further complicated as rapid expansion of current expenditures was added to the inertia of investment projects. One of the components of increased expenditure — debt service — was a victim of the very strategy employed to sustain the growth rate; the other — personnel expenses — was a reflection of the limited possibilities for wage controls in a climate of political liberalization and growing inflation.

Inflation exacerbates conflict between the public and private sectors as both compete for productive resources. Brazil's continuous expansion of the public sector destroyed a complementary relationship that had prevailed between the state and the private sector for many years. The first signs of change in this relationship emerged when it was no longer possible to sustain growth of the plethora of subsidies and incentives benefiting various parts of the business sector. A rise in the internal real interest rate became the major indication of the struggle for resources between the public and private sector. Monetary correction could no longer neutralize the allocative effects of growing inflation. Consider in addition that the international financial market abruptly closed after the trauma caused by the Mexican default. With the drastic contraction in the supply of external resources, one of the main links in the chain of growth was broken: adjustment was no longer an option; in view of effective budget limitations, it became an immediate requirement.

Compulsory Adjustment

Brazil's strategy of growth with indebtedness was not altered deliberately. There was no transition process in which events were anticipated and an adjustment alternative selected to minimize disruption of the economy. External finance stopped. Adjustment of the balance of payments had to be achieved in the absence of an international financial market. Virtually overnight, excess liquidity turned into absolute illiquidity. Frantic competition among hundreds of international banks to lend money was replaced by bureaucratic, cartel-like advisory committees.

Just as institutional rigidity caused by expansion of the state in the economy explains overborrowing by developing countries, so do predatory competition, faulty information, and externalities in the financial market help explain overlending by private banks. The level of risk was masked by rates of return well above domestic operations, and the concentration of risk was diluted by the government distributing loans among different entities of a single public sector. This distribution of loans facilitated the tie-in between credits and specific projects. The government's participation also conferred the moral comfort of government guarantees. Credit expansion proceeded without the banks' ever admitting that they were financing a balance-of-payments disequilibrium.

The Polish crisis, and particularly the Mexican shock, abruptly showed that the emperor had no clothes. The result was a converging awareness among the banks that each, and therefore the entire financial system, was overexposed in some countries and regions. The market had failed to flag those events and thus did not allow for reduction in the supply of funds to be spread out over time. The attempt to reduce drastically in a matter of months a level of exposure that had grown too high over many years meant an extreme contraction of external liquidity, with strong negative repercussions for developing countries. The limits to the liquidity squeeze were set by the survival needs of the world financial system rather than by concern for the affected countries.

Two significant conclusions may be derived from this course of events: first, given its compulsory nature, external adjustment cannot serve as an optimization process for facing economic and social constraints; it is inherently inefficient. Second, the availability of external resources will not be solved automatically through the market. Whatever one's ideological preferences, it is clear that conventional market forces no longer are working in most countries. Instead, a complex and tortuous negotiation process has been set in motion whose result depends on the relative bargaining power of each party. The solution is no longer solely economic, but increasingly political.

The Need for Megasurpluses

For debtor countries, external adjustment is the compulsory adaptation of a domestic economy to the new view of risk held by international bankers. It is tautological to talk about the success of external adjustment: the current account deficit will be reduced to the amount

TABLE 4.1 **External Adjustment** *(non-oil developing countries in US$ billion)*

	1981	1982	1983	1984	1985	1986
Trade Balance	− 82.2	− 52.5	− 23.4	− 6.2	− 4.0	− 4.7
Exports	337.3	323.1	332.4	367.6	398.0	437.5
Imports	419.5	275.6	355.8	375.8	401.9	442.3
Current Account	− 108.3	− 86.1	− 52.1	− 37.9	− 37.2	− 35.4

Source: World Bank

that can be financed. Under such conditions, the trade balance is a residual; it is the reconciliation of the service deficit (predominantly interest payments) to the availability of external loans and the net inflow of investment capital (since reserves are assumed to have been exhausted). A trade surplus is thus logically inevitable. The final adjustment must be made in imports once the maximum feasible level of exports over a given length of time is known. Not even commercial or interest payment arrears can prevent an eventual curtailment of imports. At best, such maneuvers can only delay the inevitable adjustment.

It is therefore not surprising to find that only after two years of adjustment has the current account deficit of debtor countries been drastically reduced (Table 4.1). The reduction merely reflects the formidable and extraordinary contraction of international liquidity for those countries. In following the logic of this practice to its next step, we might conclude that a further squeeze on liquidity would be an even better policy as the resulting reduction of external disequilibrium would be even greater. Proceeding logically, we would eventually arrive at the fallacy of applauding the closedown of financial markets.

Evidently, the form in which a trade surplus is generated determines the path of external adjustment and its impact on the domestic economy. In principle, the more closely the trade balance surplus is tied to export growth rather than to the reduction of imports, the more surpluses will be associated with a resumption of economic activity. Thus, external demand would have a favorable effect on production

TABLE 4.2   External Adjustment in Latin America *(US$ billion)*

	1980	1981	1982	1983	1984	1985	1986
Trade Balance	− 10.1	− 12.6	− 1.3	27.0	39.4	33.5	18.4
Imports	117.7	128.7	104.5	75.4	58.3	58.4	59.9
Exports	107.6	116.1	103.2	102.4	97.7	91.9	78.3
Current Account	− 28.1	− 40.1	− 40.9	− 7.4	− .2	− 4.0	− 14.2
Net Transfer of Resources	11.5	10.4	− 18.7	− 31.2	− 27.0	− 32.9	− 22.1
Net Transfer/ Exports (%)	10.7	9.0	− 18.1	− 30.5	− 23.7	− 30.2	− 23.2
Interest/Exports (%)	20.2	28.0	41.0	36.0	35.6	35.2	35.1
Debt/Exports (%)	214	248	321	343	322	342	401

Source: Economic Commission for Latin America, ECLA

and employment levels—true in Brazil as of 1984–1986.

One must consider whether it is possible to sustain an accumulation of megasurpluses over time without needing to restrain imports artificially. Given the unpredictable behavior of exports—largely dependent on world economic trends—the need to generate surpluses continuously requires the permanent practice of import substitution. Even in a diverse economy such as Brazil's, economic and technological barriers to substitution do exist. In countries that are net food importers, substitution is simply impossible, as it is limited by domestic agricultural capacity (Table 4.2).

It is difficult to foresee the longer-term consequences of such external adjustment on the ability of LDCs to absorb and incorporate technological changes such as those under way in the more industrialized countries. Technological obsolescence may affect our external competitiveness and limit the potential growth of exports. In many nontraditional sectors, Brazil has gained in world markets as a result of state-of-the-art technology aided by the import of physical capital. The automotive industry is a good example. A growing space for continuing import expansion is therefore critical for development.

Even in those sectors where substitution by domestic production is economically feasible—pulp and paper, steel and oil are remarkable

TABLE 4.3   **Internal Adjustment in Latin America** *(percent)*

	1981	1982	1983	1984	1985	1986
Real Rates of Growth (GDP)	0.5	− 1.4	− 2.4	3.2	2.7	3.4
Real Per-Capita Growth	− 1.9	− 3.7	− 4.7	0.9	0.4	1.2
Inflation	58.2	84.8	131.1	185.2	275.3	69.1

Source: Economic Commision for Latin American, ECLA

examples in Brazil — time is an important constraint. In the oil industry, it was ten years from the first OPEC price increase until domestic production covered a significant share of total consumption. Over that period, the alternative was to finance the additional burden through external borrowing and slashing non-oil imports. Long maturation periods apply to other sectors, too. As import substitution takes hold, there is always a period of time during which some measure of domestic protection must be applied. Limiting competition results in inflation, directly by affecting production costs, and indirectly by raising expectations (Table 4.3).

When the financial market was functioning regularly, elimination of trade balance deficits was enough to restore the equilibrium of balance of payments and even allow for the accumulation of reserves. Under current conditions, market forces no longer exist, and the supply of external resources is determined independently by international banks in an attempt to minimize their exposure in debtor countries. Equilibrium of external accounts thus requires continuous generation of megasurpluses. For the accumulation of surpluses to ensure the viability of the process from the viewpoint of servicing the debt, the growth of exports must necessarily be higher than the external interest rate.

To keep exports growing not only at a *positive* pace but always *above* the level of interest rates demands either a series of highly favorable external conditions or the aggressive use of domestic instruments that will stimulate exportable production, especially the exchange rate. Sustaining a permanent real devaluation in the exchange rate introduces an inflationary bias domestically, in addition to exerting strong pressure on the economy's real interest rates. It is one of the major links between external and internal disequilibrium.

Reversal of the Net Flow of Resources

The adjustment-without-liquidity approach inevitably leads to a continuous net transfer of resources abroad. This is true even under the best possible conditions, i.e., megasurpluses sustained over time and in such a way that the growth in exports is systematically over and above the external interest rate.

Developing countries have historically been net capital importers. The change to exporter obviously is not the result of a deliberate reduction of external debt, as would be expected with advancement to higher economic stages. It is simply a reflection of the simultaneous action of a drastic contraction in the supply of foreign credit and a sharp rise in external interest rates. It is an expression of the ambivalent attitude of banks as they insist on the application of market conditions in a nonmarket context.

The reduction in new resources from the banks is not offset by other institutional sources such as the IMF, the World Bank, the IDB, or government loans. Industrialized governments that hope for a spontaneous solution to the debt crisis have reacted slowly. They avoid any commitment of long-term resources, even to replenish the capital base of multilateral institutions. The evolution of external interest rates remains unpredictable as rates float in the wake of discretionary measures taken by the United States in managing its domestic policies.

As currently enforced, external adjustment represents an accommodation of the balance of payments to a given volume of financing determined almost unilaterally by the international banks. The favorable effect of export expansion on the domestic economy, in cases — such as in Brazil—where such expansion is feasible is offset by the negative impact on investment capacity represented by a net outflow of resources. Inflation is aggravated by the expectation of exchange devaluations, permanent pressure on the prices of tradeable goods, and the reduced domestic competitiveness caused by import restrictions.

It is crucial to understand that a change in the terms of debt rescheduling is vital not only to assure more effective adjustment of the balance of payments, but also to help implement an internal adjustment process with less negative consequences for real output.

Internal Adjustment

The decision to implement or delay internal adjustment is basically political. As in the external sector, it is always possible to finance internal disequilibrium by printing money or increasing indebtedness for a time. The ultimate limitation is the willingness of the central bank to issue more money, i.e., to finance the government by an inflation tax. In the institutional framework of the central banks in most developing countries, financing the public deficit through the issuance of currency is usually close to automatic.[3] This strategy turns the money supply into an endogenous variable beyond the effective control of monetary authorities.

Successful internal adjustment is reflected in the ability to reconcile deflation and economic growth within a relatively short time. In Brazil it has been difficult to achieve. Since the mid-1970s we have witnessed the escalation of inflation followed by economic slowdown. In the first months of 1987, the tie between rampant inflation and a fall in economic activity has become stronger. It is not yet clear when this sad marriage will end (Table 4.4).

The Brazilian experience of the past few years illustrates that correction of internal imbalances is more complex than was apparent at first. In considering the management of aggregate demand, it is essential to understand first that in economic policy, the order of factors does affect the outcome. Although the correction of key macro prices (exchange and fuels, for example) is vital for the achievement of allocative gains, the timeliness of implementation and the way in which short-term policies (monetary, fiscal, wage) are combined will make a huge difference in the behavior of inflation and in the possibilities for renewed growth. The usual series of government actions to correct internal imbalances prolongs the period of adjustment and amplifies the negative consequences for real product. In nearly all developing countries, revi-

TABLE 4.4   External Adjustment: Latin America's Main Debtors

	Current Account (US$ billion)					
	1981	1982	1983	1984	1985	1986
Brazil	− 11.7	− 14.8	− 6.2	+ 05	+ 0.3	− 2.8
Mexico	− 13.9	− 6.2	+ 5.5	+ 4.2	+ 0.4	− 3.5
Argentina	− 4.7	− 2.4	− 2.4	− 2.5	− 1.0	− 2.4

	Interest/Exports (%)					
	1981	1982	1983	1984	1985	1986
Brazil	40.4	57.1	43.5	39.7	40.0	37.7
Mexico	29.0	47.3	37.5	39.0	36.0	40.0
Argentina	35.5	53.6	58.4	57.6	51.1	51.8

Source: Economic Commission for Latin America, ECLA

sion of key macro prices takes the form of substantial and erratic increases, which have a major impact on costs and indirect, lasting consequences for general price levels due to the change in expectations. In fact, renewed expectations, along with the realignment of relative prices, render the classic distinction between a "once-and-for-all" and "permanent" price increase meaningless in practice.[4]

In the case of Brazil, generalized indexation makes for a nearly automatic transformation of specific price readjustments into across-the-board increases. To prevent this would require implementing restrictive fiscal and monetary policies in advance of the adjustments, which rarely occurs. The result is a speedup of inflation that makes it politically impossible to attempt restriction through wage controls afterward.

These macro price discontinuities have a direct effect on the public debt service, making it increasingly difficult to control current spending. Again we find that in a framework of strong inflationary pressures, it is seldom possible to offset such effects through wage controls. The margin for fiscal maneuvering is limited to tax increases and curtailment of public investment, both of which impede economic growth. Generally speaking, even deep real cuts in investment are not enough to offset the expansion of public spending. Monetary restriction is the only means to prevent uncontrollable inflation.

The application of monetary brakes in a scenario of expansionary fiscal policies and wage rigidity places a disproportionate burden on interest rates during the adjustment process. A sharp rise in real interest rates is unavoidable, and becomes a major barrier to resumption of private investment. Public expenditures accelerate through an increase in debt service in a process similar to what happens during an exchange adjustment.

The level of real interest rates needed to break down inflationary expectations is normally beyond the capacity not only of the private sector, but of the financial system itself. The sustainable interest rate is an objective limitation to the success of the monetary alternative, which explains the paradox of monetary policy over the past few years: tight money raised interest rate levels high enough to stop expansion of the private sector, but not enough to reverse inflation.[5]

Process Distortions

Brazil's recent experience is more than sufficient to illustrate the conflicts I have described. To correct external disequilibrium, the exchange rate was readjusted sharply in February 1982. As in late 1979, this new maxi-devaluation was implemented against a background of growing public expenditures and full wage indexation, feeding inflationary expectations that were translated into price acceleration. Halfway through the year, additional macro price corrections were implemented (for fuel and wheat, for instance), as required for allocative efficiency. These in turn reinforced inflationary expectations, as public spending continued to grow despite substantial cuts in investment levels.

Unrestrained inflation was only prevented by tightening money. That did not, however, prevent prices from settling at a higher plateau. The result was strong pressure on internal interest rates, dampening the economy and making it difficult to resume growth. Therefore, any attempt to offset rigid nominal wages and a loose fiscal policy through tightening the money supply prevent hyperinflation at the cost of higher interest rates. The conflict between the objectives of fighting inflation and preserving economic activity is aggravated.

Monetary correction has turned from hero to villain in the Brazilian economy. Indexation was introduced in Brazil as a tool against inflation, as it allowed financing the public deficit through selling long-term public bonds.[6] In the period 1964–1974, monetary correction was not an obstacle to the reduction of inflation and gradual resumption of growth, because there were no exogenous shocks, and public accounts were kept under control. It played its allocative role with outstanding neutrality.

Difficulties became apparent in 1974, when the first oil shock had to be absorbed internally. From then on, destabilizing factors came into play that could not be totally offset by direct adjustment of the price indexes (i.e., excluding from the indexes "accidental" price variations). In 1979 there were two added complications: discontinuous exchange readjustments and extension of full indexation to all wages and salaries. New internal shocks ensued, related to the elimination of subsidies. Thus, precisely when substantial changes were being introduced in macro prices, the rippling effect of those changes was multiplied by the general application of indexation.

It would be naive to imagine that a mere change in the method of measuring monetary correction or its phaseout pure and simple would be sufficient to bring about substantial changes in the behavior of inflation. A comprehensive set of measures and reforms is required to produce in-depth changes in the formation of expectations and thus to rebuild the foundation for a positive adjustment of the Brazilian economy. Modifications in the monetary correction system should be designed to reflect such a new economic framework.

In February 1986, the Cruzado plan was implemented, placing a general freeze on all prices, wages, and the exchange rate. The basic mistake of the plan was to diagnose Brazilian inflation as pure inertia fed only by monetary correction. Since public deficit kept growing and interest rates were pegged at an artificially low level, the result was an explosion of consumption that soon led to enormous distortions. Black markets developed everywhere, and already in October excess aggregate demand spilled over into external accounts, resulting in a sharp decline in trade surpluses and a substantial loss of international reserves (about $4 billion). In early 1987, price controls had to be eliminated. Inflation exploded to record levels (25 percent per month), leaving Brazil with a regressive combination of rising prices and recession.

Some Requirements for a New Strategy

The changes experienced over the past ten years have been so profound that we can no longer ignore them or imagine that solutions can be found in the institutional *status quo*, internally or externally. There has been a radical change in the world economy energy matrix, followed by an explosion of interest rates and a shock to the international financial markets. To think that such a scenario can be resolved by the unilateral adjustment efforts of developing countries is profoundly unfair and economically ineffective. Internally, deep qualitative and quantitative changes have taken place in Brazil's public sector as its role has shifted from development leader to a major source of economic disequilibrium.

For Brazil as for many LDCs, the first years of this decade have been marked by dangerously spiraling inflation and either recession or limited growth, in contrast to the early 1970s' golden era of rapid expansion. Such an outcome was a strong blow to the emerging belief that Brazilian development had reached a self-sustained stage and was becoming more or less automatic. Those optimistic expectations have vanished in the violent wake of recent changes. We have entered a world of expensive energy, limited external finance, and unstable growth. Domestically the economy is increasingly rigid because of the omnipresence of the state, aggravated by obsolescent institutions and instruments. These structural changes have left a deep imprint from which new terms of reference have begun to emerge, and where the issue of economic development has to be addressed differently.

Redefinition must necessarily include the external issue. In the current framework, a country is forced to generate megasurpluses in its trade balance, in turn introducing an inflationary bias via exchange expectations and limiting its growth potential through the transfer of domestic savings abroad. The problem is that this strategy does not ensure an adequate solution to external indebtedness *per se*. The two main issues were not yet effectively approached: how to reestablish the supply of external funds at levels consistent with the resumption of growth; and how to reduce the vulnerability of the balance of payments to external shocks such as interest rate fluctuations.

It is unrealistic to expect overnight solutions for either of these crucial problems: in a nonmarket situation there is no automatic mechanism for reconciling the interests of debtor countries and private banks. The current real level of external interest rates does not represent a long-term equilibrium. Those rates reflect the anticipated behavior of the United States' public deficit, over which developing countries have no say. The unpredictable behavior of interest rates is an element of uncertainty that cannot be offset by gains in the trade balance. Fluctuation in external interest rates is the major element of vulnerability in the current agreements between debtor countries and commercial banks. All present rescheduling schemes can become unrealistic overnight based on the performance of interest rates alone.

The objective of the banks is to reduce their exposure to a minimum, which necessarily leads to a drastic cut in the supply of new credit. This credit squeeze is limited solely by the stability of the financial system.

Nothing can ensure *a priori* consistency between the volume of external resources thus defined and the actual needs of the countries determined on the basis of a minimum expected growth rate. It seems evident that there is no way the two can converge spontaneously.

It may be argued that repeated good performance by the trade balance will gradually bring about a voluntary comeback of market lending. This belief is unrealistic, as it does not distinguish between the adjustment of flows and of stocks: trade surpluses reduce the need for additional resources and therefore affect the pace of indebtedness, but they cannot alter the inherited debt stock, which will continue to affect bank risk decisively. Banks are now realistically internalizing losses and raising capital and reserves, which will place a still more selective stamp on the availability of new credit.

The concept of multiyear rescheduling introduced by the banks initially for Mexico and now for other countries confirms the foregoing assumptions. Rescheduling will not by itself reverse the trend toward a net outflow of financial resources, which is becoming a permanent and chronic regressive pattern.

Long-term debt restructuring must be carried out to establish a logical relationship between sustainable external adjustment and the renewal of growth. It requires setting long-term parameters: long-term shadow interest rates and a minimum growth rate for external credit linked to realistic targets for the growth of real domestic product. It is essential that the supply of external resources be dealt with side-by-side with the question of interest rates. Introduction of the concept of the long-term shadow interest rate as the relevant reference rate for external debt rescheduling would signify a profound change from the present system, in which market conditions are applied to a nonmarket situation. The basic assumption of the proposed policy is that current interest rates are not equilibrium rates; quite the opposite, they reflect the internal disequilibrium of the American economy. Over time it is reasonable to assume that current rates will converge to the long-term equilibrium level.[7]

The relevant interest for long-term rescheduling is by definition the shadow rate, which retains a market reference without the speculation-based "noise" of current rates. Given sufficient time, effective rates should hover around the shadow rate, and differences both positive and negative should cancel out. For the scheme to work, a refinancing mechanism is required for the differential; it would reconcile the gap between current bank returns, which would stay tied to prevailing market rates and interest expense incurred by the countries, which would then be computed with the reference rate as a basis. Determination of a minimum growth rate for new loans under the framework of multiyear rescheduling would break the regressive nature of the international banks' decisions. Such a commitment is vital to reduce uncertainties on the external side by curtailing exchange speculation and minimizing the flight of private capital. It also can be reconciled with the banks' objective of reducing exposure in debtor countries, but only if it is implemented gradually rather than suddenly. A growth rate for additional credit no higher than the expected growth in the banks' capital base would be enough: it would allow the availability of long-term new money to debtor LDCs to be matched to a relative decrease in the share of assets these loans represent in bank portfolios.

The expected GDP growth rate needs to be defined in order to meet social goals (which assume an increase in real per capita income), but it also needs to take into account concrete internal constraints (the fight against inflation) and external limitations (a tolerable level of current account deficit). External parameters then must be defined so as not to become obstacles to achievement of the target growth rate. That does not mean, of course, that the product growth target is assured simply as a result of greater freedom on the external battlefront. It means only that changes must be introduced in the debt negotiations. Growth no longer can be treated as a residual left to fluctuate at the whim of external conditions.

Multilateral organizations and governments must commit themselves to cover any persisting differential between bank credit as defined above and minimum country needs estimated on the basis of a given growth target. The assurance of long-term external financing would still depend on a continuing adjustment effort by developing country economies. Actually, as those countries once again become net capital importers — as reserves accumulate faster and external vulnerability is reduced — the new strategy will make the correction of disequilibrium more feasible and longer lasting. Any solution to the problem requires active participation by the governments of industrialized countries, but that is a natural development of the entire negotiation process in an acknowledgedly nonmarket situation. This is a typical case in which government action is needed to reestablish a functioning market over time. A return to the market will be possible only if we eliminate once and for all the specter of expected capital losses that has threatened international finance since the Mexican shock.

One virtue of using the approach of partial capitalization of interest is that it forces government intervention and ensures long-term commitment to preventing the destabilization of the financial system that might result from a sharp fall in bank profitability. At the same time, the faster current equilibrium interest rates converge, the faster special support schemes such as the interest facility will be superseded by events.[8] Thus, a major attraction of the capitalization approach is that it creates an objective stimulus for developed countries, especially the United States, to adjust their own economies.

Multiyear definition of a minimum supply of new money and application of a reference interest rate would set a sound basis for long-term rescheduling, and this would differ widely from the current approach, in which an expected decline in the ratio of "new money to interest payment," is stimulating the proliferation of unilateral actions by debtor countries.

For many LDCs, reduction of the annual flow of interest payments combined with funds provided by multilateral organizations would suffice for external adjustment to be compatible with renewed leeway for internal growth. Prior commitment to a minimum amount of funds would eliminate the uncertainty about external liquidity. This risk has been one of the limiting factors in the resumption of private investment in developing economies.

The new parameters for external credit expansion and interest rate levels may be interpreted as anticipating a natural trend into which market forces would converge, provided these forces were effectively at work. Contraction of external credit has gone much further than reasonable, even in view of the need to reduce the external disequilibria of developing countries. It rather reflects a faulty attempt at self-protection by each financial institution, which ultimately might have led to destabilization of the entire financial system as a result of the compound effect of externalities, had not a new exogenous force (central banks and the IMF) intervened. Definition of a minimum growth for new resources therefore restores the equilibrium between adjustment and liquidity. Similarly, the uncomfortable consequences of erratic fluctuations of external rates, currently the cause of added uncertainties because of their unpredictable behavior, would be eliminated.

Application of these principles would reverse the current situation, which has turned developing countries into net capital exporters. A trade balance surplus would not be a target *per se*, forcibly generated to accommodate the economy to unilaterally determined liquidity levels. In fact, greater availability of external funds would enable the balance of trade to follow a behavior pattern more in line with economic growth needs and inflation control.

The Relationship Between External and Internal Adjustment

A major change in the terms of external rescheduling would set the basis for more effective *internal* adjustment. Expansion of the margins for decision making on the external front and elimination of the risk of a new liquidity crunch would have an immediate and positive impact on the flow of foreign investment, and would help reverse net disinvestment by the private sector, one of the blackest marks of the

TABLE 4.5   Brazil: Internal Adjustment *(percent)*

	1981	1982	1983	1984	1985	1986
Real Rate of Growth (GDP)	– 3.4	0.9	– 2.5	5.7	8.3	8.6
Rate of Inflation	95.2	99.7	211.0	223.8	235.0	65.0
Money Supply	69.9	86.8	89.1	201.9	304.3	303.8
Public Deficit (% of GDP)	12.5	15.8	18.5	23.3	27.8	9.9
Real Interest Rate	12.20	15.25	15.25	20.30	20.30	4.6
Rate of Exchange (Rate of Change)	95.1	97.7	289.4	223.6	229.5	41.9
Real Wage (Rate of Change)	12.6	4.0	– 2.2	– 5.0	3.1	7.0
Unemployment Rate	8.0	6.3	6.7	7.2	5.0	3.6

Source: Getulio Vargas Foundation (GVF)

current external crisis. There would be a reduction of inflationary bias, associated with forced megasurpluses. Should surpluses occur, they would be the natural outcome of internal efficiency and competitiveness allied with favorable external conditions, but never a corollary of the artificial containment of imports or an excessive incentive to export.

Trade surpluses thus generated would be directed to a more rapid accumulation of reserves rather than to the payment of interest abroad. There would be greater freedom to manipulate the exchange policy in order to encourage exports without feeding inflation. The possibility of implementing a less aggressive exchange policy, i.e., no longer having to assure a continuous real devaluation combined with a reduction of external interest rates on the stock of rescheduled debt, would have a favourable impact on the internal structure of interest rates (Table 4.5).[9]

The existence of a high stock of external resources already in the country and available for relending would act to reduce internal rates. Expectations of a more moderate exchange devaluation also would help domestic interest rates. Finally, there would be a direct impact on the public debt service, with favorable reverberations and relief of the demand for credit.

If we add the permanent contribution of increased investment capacity through reallocation of domestic net resources currently transferred overseas, a clear picture emerges of how much a change in the terms of rescheduling would mean. It would be instrumental in generating effective conditions for a positive adjustment of the Brazilian economy.

The internal counterpart of lower interest rates is a decrease in the service burden of the public sector, helping to speed up the reduction of the overall deficit. To the extent that a continuous effort is made to cut public investment fat and other special current expenditures, there would be a gradual but steady reversal of the private sector crowding. The favorable impact of debt restructuring also would extend to the private sector by creating objective conditions for a resumption of investment.

The current method of correcting internal imbalances would change. So far, control of aggregate demand has relied solely on continuous increases in real interest rates, the major indication of the conflict between public deficit rigidity and monetary restraint. The consequences have been drastic: a fall in public and private investment with no corresponding reduction in the overall public deficit. In fact, statistics show growth in the public deficit for two years following the agreement with the IMF. The inevitable outcome is continuing inflationary pressure and stunted growth.

The new external debt negotiation terms described here would set the basis for an adjustment process with declining real interest rates. It is the only means to establish a logical link between short-term changes and structural adjustment, while preserving investment levels. Thus a socially feasible relationship between short- and long-term goals would be established.

There can be no adjustment with growth without private investment, the major victim of internal and external uncertainties built up over the last five years. To idle our capacity and then allow it to be used in response to the spastic behavior of demand does not qualify as economic growth, let alone resumption of development. That was an important lesson of the frustrating Cruzado plan. The extraordinary expansion of aggregate demand in 1986 could not be taken as a basis for renewed investment, because it was caused by artificial increases in real wages through a price freeze and negative interest rates, while public sector imbalances kept expanding. Anticipated inflationary pressures, which came alive in 1987, has offset any significant expansion of private investment.

Changing Expectations

The Brazilian economy needs a real shock to change negative expectations that will represent a true break between past and future. In an environment of high and rising inflation, sound development is inviable. On the other hand, debt negotiations similar to those of recent years maintain uncertainty about future liquidity, setting additional limitations on growth.

A new element must be introduced to reverse these expectations: a clear and unmistakable change in the terms of eternal renegotiation, which explicitly introduces matters such as new loans, interest rates, and even a reduction in the debt stock itself. The development of a secondary debt market, where prices of these assets are quoted, may soon lead to the viable substitution of a "new" reduced debt, such as long-term bonds, with an objective guarantee (a certain proportion of a country's reserve) for present outstanding "old" debt. Inasmuch as such changes would sign a fast fall on public spending, they would also help to change domestic expectations with respect to both inflation and private investment.

External flexibility would need to be amplified internally by a wide range of reforms that would ultimately return control of the state to society. Redirection of the public deficit would no longer be just a budgetary question, but the driving force behind institutional reorganization of the Brazilian economy.

Historical examples from several countries and from our own economy clearly show that inflation can be curbed and growth resumed once society finds that basic sources of disequilibrium have been effectively modified. A shift in expectations caused by concrete action on imbalances in itself causes reversal of the inflationary trend. The control of German, Hungarian, Austrian, and Polish inflation following World War I was nearly immediate in response to the announcement of a stabilization program.[10]

In the 1920s the League of Nations played a role similar to that of the IMF today: it extended loans to improve liquidity in connection with a stabilization program centered on control of the public deficit. Implementation of the internal adjustment program was followed by an in-depth revision of the terms of payment for war reparations. External debts were renegotiated so they would not harm economic recovery. In the 1940s the Marshall Plan implemented the idea of positive adjustment: correction of internal disequilibrium was achieved under conditions of favorable external liquidity and indeed with a massive net inflow of capital.

Two basic factors underlie the positive shock to expectations: the enhancement of internal credibility and the modification of the terms for renegotiation of external debt. Internal credibility was brought about by institutional reform: an independent central bank was created, and a law was passed to forbid the funding of indiscriminate budgetary spending through money issues. Substantial improvement of terms on the external debt worked with the internal reforms to provide the needed shock. The simultaneous implementation of these structural changes in the external and internal frameworks help explain the successful reversal of inflation and the later resumption of development.

Brazil did something similar in 1964: a set of profound internal reforms was implemented, including tax reform and the creation of what was intended to be an independent central bank; favorable external conditions allowed the country to become a net capital importer. Over the next few years inflation slowed and development resumed.

In contrast, in 1986, instead of addressing the basic sources of internal imbalance, and particularly of the public deficit, there was a frustrating series of efforts at fighting inflation through a wide range of price and wage controls.

Brazil today is suffering from a classic demand inflation, the main source of which is a public deficit, growing not only at the federal level but also in states and municipalities. Compulsory wage indexation makes it extremely difficult to reduce inflation without having a serious impact on real output and employment. In this situation, only the simultaneous reformulation of external conditions and implementation of comprehensive internal reforms can reestablish adjustment with growth. It is an error to imagine that external renegotiation alone can bring about economic recovery. Likewise, it would be impossible to lay the groundwork for growth exclusively on the basis of internal adjustment. Regardless of political constraints, such an attempt would come up against the logical contradiction between external accommodation and inflationary tension.

A New Institutional Framework

The current situation clearly calls for a comprehensive set of reforms as part of a new institutional framework. Confronting the Brazilian public deficit is primarily a matter of redefining power. Overcentralization of the decisionmaking process surely helps explain the trend observed in recent years toward self-fostered enlargement of the public sector.

Congress should take over effective control of major spending decisions now centralized in the executive branch. Episodic attempts to curb the public deficit in Brazil have led nearly always to a passive fiscal policy, where increased public spending is supported simply by a rise in taxation. Reform of the public sector must be undertaken on the basis of legal restrictions to stop new expenditures not supported by defined resources. This devolution of economic decisionmaking power is a natural counterpart to the institutionalization of democracy underway in the political sphere.[11]

There should be a unified budget for the country and a simple monetary program whereby growth targets for the key monetary aggregates are set to stabilize overall price levels. *Unification of the budget will eliminate the oddity of a monetary budget. The public deficit will become entirely transparent while executive and legislative branches reach a consensus on how to ensure its control on a permanent basis. Such a process goes beyond budget consolidation, enlarging the concept of government expenditure to include total public expenses, even those disguised in the nooks and crannies of the monetary budget and in the maze of state agencies and public corporations.*

Subsidies of all types should be defined side-by-side with conventional (current and capital) expenses, both for the federal government and state corporations. *Deficit management no longer should be a privilege of technocrats, but a political process in which conflicting interests are settled. This change would generate responsibility by the whole society, through legal representatives, in the fundamental issue of the state's role in the economy.*

Articulation between the state and society via politics does not necessarily assure a reduction of the public sector's weight in the economy: in some countries political decentralization goes hand-in-hand with an economically powerful state. What political articulation does forestall, however, is the self-expansion of the public sector, i.e., its endogenous and discretionary growth without previous sanction by society. Under the suggested economic and political framework, the possibilities for unilateral state action are minimized. The rules of the economic system should be legislatively ratified, rather than resulting from bureaucratic acts alone.

Following budgetary consolidation, elimination of the major sources of deficit and reallocation of economic responsibility between the executive and the legislature is imperative to give the central bank more freedom to act. This means independence that is broad and deep; it means an equal distance from the executive and legislative branches; and it implies the legal responsibility to stabilize overall price levels. It therefore involves a limitation on financing government overspending by the issuing of currency and abdication of the senseless hope that development can be carried out through the management of monetary policy.

Actions by the central bank may sometimes be at odds with other government policies. To preserve their central banks from the pressure of vested interests, many countries have set them up as independent agencies. A legal cocoon helps them to reconcile differences between plans and resources. It is an ingenious mechanism invented by democratic societies in order to constrain themselves. An independent central bank is an institution created to say *no*, a word not easily spoken by the government itself.[12]

In the foregoing pattern, reform of the public sector will allow a better definition of constraints in the domestic economy, which will help to achieve economic targets. Where the public deficit no longer can be financed automatically by issuing money, borrowing, or taxing, it becomes mandatory to reopen discussions on the state's role in the economy. In other words, an institutional approach to the public deficit will forcibly lead to a broad redefinition of the state's functions and responsibilities.

In this regard, while the latest debt crisis has disclosed the existence of real and unavoidable external and internal constraints, it has also highlighted the key role that allocative efficiency may play in the development process. In the private sector, the shift in relative capital and economic costs has induced a natural relocation of productive resources away from industries artificially fostered by subsidies and incentives toward areas of comparative advantage. This has meant a healthy rediscovery of growth potential in sectors such as agriculture and mining, given their second-best treatment during the years of "industrialization at any cost." Likewise, the public sector has been forced to review the concept of economies of scale, often misused to justify large-scale projects of dubious social benefit. The wider dispersion of investments is an unavoidable consequence not only of economic limitations, but also of the decentralization of decisionmaking. It is the only way to reconcile the state's role as productive agent with its role as social agent.

The shock of expectations resulting from a sudden improvement in projections of the public deficit and profound changes in the terms of external rescheduling would create the conditions needed to break the cycle of inflation and reactivate investment. Following a shift in expectations, the process would gain its own momentum: prices would decrease more than the money supply would grow, and liquidity would increase in real terms. Decline in the public deficit would reduce the need for state financing and improve the outlook for interest rates. Reduced interest rates and a slowdown of inflation would in turn diminish uncertainty and extend the investment horizon for the private sector. Existing liquid resources currently held back for short-term applications would then be released for productive investment. Add to this the gains in efficiency associated with improved allocation of private and public resources, thanks to a realignment of relative prices as well as the institutional reforms discussed above. Once the risk of external constraints is eliminated through a long-term supply of resources and predictable interest rates, internal momentum will suffer no more interruptions: the economy will be back on the track of self-sustained growth.

Indexation in the New Framework

Only after a profound change in expectations has been triggered by the announced institutional revisions would the economic and political framework be set for phasing out indexation. Without first eliminating the sources of disequilibrium, it would be naive to think that indexation changes alone would help control inflation or reactivate the economy. The 1980 attempt at partial disindexation of exchange and financial assets is a glaring example of the difficulties encountered in such a strategy. In terms of exchange, a new, more flexible approach cannot be envisaged without a preliminary change in the terms of external rescheduling and eliminating of the requirement to generate mega-surpluses. It is equally risky to alter indexation rules for voluntary savings under growing inflation. Countless attempts show the result to be the flight of capital from financial assets into real assets, thus rekindling inflation.

The Cruzado plan, implemented in 1986, presents crystal-clear evidence for these points. Indexation of savings was eliminated without assuring effective control of the basic sources of inflation. As a result, there was a drastic fall in voluntary savings, and personal resources were redirected to consumption, the stock market, or the purchase of foreign currency.[13]

It makes no sense to use partial wage disindexation as a tool for bringing down inflation. The effects of such an isolated measure on expectations are modest, and the fall in real wages that follows inflation soon renders this alternative politically unworkable, as illustrated by the ups and downs of Brazilian wage policy over the past five years. Attempts to control wages have been frustrated by persistent inflation fed by growth of the public deficit. Conditions must first be created to ensure the reversal of inflation, and only then to break the connection between wage readjustment and past price increases.

To try to obtain real wage gains through legislation without attention to inflation is equally absurd. Such overindexation inevitably leads to the explosion of inflation, as illustrated so clearly by recent developments in Argentina and Brazil.

When the needed internal and external reforms have been announced, monetary correction can be eliminated gradually and painlessly. Changes in expectations will allow a clear break between past and future price behavior. Exchange correction can be instituted on the basis of floating rates, leaving aside mechanical rules and allowing the market to anticipate the positive impact of lowered inflation on external accounts.

For savings, the current form of *a posteriori* indexation would be maintained only for long-term assets and liabilities, just to cover the transition until reality begins to confirm expectations. For the short- and medium-term, market rates would prevail, not as a result of government decision, but from the market's evaluation of the prospects for inflation. If the market is not convinced that inflation will fall, it makes no sense to force such expectations by manipulating monetary correction indices; that is an exercise in futility that affects government credibility. On the other hand, once the expectation shock occurs, the market probably will adjust the new inflation forecasts faster and more efficiently than would the government itself.

Similarly, following a change in expectations, for the determination of wages it would suffice to eliminate the mandatory requirement of automatic correction based on past inflation, giving room to free negotiations. Throughout the past twenty years, the basic contradiction has been in trying to apply a uniform approach to wages in the diversified and heterogeneous Brazilian labor market. Market-driven wage levels are the economic counterpart to the political opening ensuring free trade unions the right to strike.[14]

Disindexation is not a magic formula to reverse Brazil's chronic inflation overnight without affecting its roots; it must be adapted to the new circumstances generated by the institutional reforms described. Such adaptation need not be traumatic; it can be a building block for positive adjustment. Monetary reform would not in itself have the power to modify expectations of inflation. Monetary reform involves only a change in the way we measure monetary values, and it would fast become obsolete should inflation persist. As it has been used in other countries, monetary reform can be ancillary to the effective reversal of inflation. It cannot be a substitute for the set of reforms discussed.[15]

By mid-1987, a new stabilization program was announced in Brazil—the Bresser plan, named for the new finance minister—with a more rational framework. The cruzeiro-dollar exchange rate was devalued by 9.6 percent, wheat subsidies were cut, and the prices of such basic public goods as gasoline, alcohol, and electricity were raised. Countless new public investments were postponed. A commitment was also made to maintain positive real interest rates in order to preserve levels of voluntary savings and discourage consumer speculation. Moreover, an attempt was made to unify the three often conflicting budgets—federal, monetary, and state enterprises. Prices and wages were frozen for just ninety days, with the promise of being liberalized gradually as inflation is controlled.

The overall plan, therefore, has some, but not all of the elements that we have discussed. It still lacks a set of basic institutional reforms that would impose legal limits on the government's ability to spend, and it does not increase the efficiency of the present tax system. These items, as we have seen, are fundamental to assuring that the new targets for the public deficit (3.5 percent of GDP in 1987 and 2.2 percent in 1988) will be achieved. Given recent failures, a simple announcement of plans to cut down the public deficit is not enough to change inflationary expectations.

The new plan, despite its imperfections, does have the merit of avoiding the dangerous trend toward hyperinflation. With its coherent trade policy—allowing for export growth—it also creates the conditions for a recovery in the balance of trade. Only time will prove whether the slowdown of prices was simply a transitory outcome or an indicator of a more permanent turnaround.

In the meantime, the new plan has set a strategy for debt negotiations that is in line with the suggestion presented in this book: the automatic refinancing of interest payments (60 percent in 1988), rather than seeking new money from private banks. Brazil is trying to start a new stage of negotiations without the formal presence of the IMF, which would assure a steady flow of external finance consistent with

minimum targets of economic growth (6 percent in 1968). The odds
of achieving a breakthrough on the debt front will vary proportionally to the successful implementation of the program, particularly with
respect to the public deficits targets. Otherwise, we will enter into an
economic turbulence with rising inflation, slow growth, and a prolonged moratorium on external payments.

Microadjustment

The adjustment process must extend all the way down to the corporate
level. The rationale for this is similar to that for long-term foreign debt
rescheduling: restructuring of corporate funding sources is vital to reducing overdependence on short-term borrowing. The fall of real market
interest rates following relief of the public sector burden will facilitate
reduction of the unfavorable marginal debt/equity ratios prevailing in
domestic corporations, especially among state enterprises. However,
definitive adjustment will demand a change in *average* debt/equity
ratios. In practical terms, this means that mechanisms must be created
to facilitate capitalization of part of the debt stock.

Restructuring will be in some part spontaneous, as the equity securities market responds to the stimulus provided by the elimination of
subsidized credit. Tax policy changes to enhance the payment of corporate dividends may reinforce the trend.

The most promising mechanism, however, is debt for equity swaps.
As I have explained before, developing countries' difficulties in servicing their debts, even after rescheduling and internalization of losses
by banks, provides a tremendous incentive for debt conversion. In fact,
in recent years an active secondary market for country papers has developed, indicating that many banks are now willing to trade some of these
assets at a discount. That creates the opportunity for potential investors to benefit from a true market stimulus, raising funds at a substantially lower cost.

The debt/equity swap may thus bridge the uncertainties that are
keeping the Age of Debt from becoming a new and promising Age of
Capital. Countries with an open policy toward foreign investment may
use this new possibility to speed the process of capitalization.

Debt/equity swaps also may be applied to enlarge the scale of domestic stock markets, expanding the capital base of corporations through the issuing of shares. Finally, because of the extra benefit of a natural hedge against exchange risks, swaps are naturally geared toward export-oriented activities, with additional favorable effects on the trade balance.

Paralleling macroeconomic patterns, corporate debt rescheduling and capitalization would generate the freedom needed for self-sustained expansion. Positive real interest rates (though on a downward trend) would discourage overborrowing to finance the new growth spurt. Such in-depth financial restructuring would supplement major changes under way on the production side of companies in response to the new relative cost matrix, particularly for manpower and energy costs.

Conclusions

There is a real risk that some countries will react to current external constraints by following an autocratic growth pattern—expanding trade barriers and further restricting capital flows. Although this strategy may seem attractive in the short run, over the long run it will narrow the possibilities for sustained development. Externally it means waiving the benefits associated with new production and consumption, represented by access to international trade. It also leads to a technological gap, limiting the potential for economic growth. Internally the counterpart of autocratic growth is increasing encroachment of the state in the economy and the stifling of private initiative. The external debt crisis then can lead to the virtual disappearance of infant market economies, which have developed shakily in Latin America these past twenty years. The financial crisis is thus converted into a development crisis.

Under the alternative approach suggested here, deliberate political action is taken to modify external and internal conditions and to correct disequilibria by building a solid market economy and stronger ties with the outside world. To accomplish this, a transition stage with intervention is needed to restore the goal of both external renegotiation and internal redefinition of the role of the state in the economy.

Recent experience proves that the economic model based on growth with indebtedness and an omnipresent state is exhausted. Any strategy for the future will have to rely on a new approach, in which the state returns to its roles as social agent, an instrument to consolidate the economic infrastructure, and, especially, a vehicle for technological innovation through the support of research. Basic research, which has been assigned a low priority in developing countries, demands direct support from the state. It is not a simple matter of replacing imported technology, but of increasing our ability to decode and absorb it. Research is also vital to the competitive exploitation of our diversified matrix of natural resources.[16]

Simultaneously, stable conditions must be created for entrepreneurial initiative and creativity, so they can become the driving force behind a new stage of development.

5

An Agenda for the Future

The external debt crisis has confronted developing countries with objective growth limitations for the first time since the golden days of the postwar era. It has disclosed the nature of internal disequilibrum, which for many years had remained hidden behind the protective cloak of rapid growth.

The roots of the crisis within each LDC lie in a unique combination of interests established in the 1970s between the state and a highly competitive and dynamic financial market. The latter has played an increasingly important role in the economy by taking control of foreign borrowing. An odd relationship between market and state—between competitiveness and inefficiency—was for some time the mainstay of the growth-with-indebtedness strategy common in Latin America until the Mexican default put an abrupt end to it. Before then, the market failed to perceive adequately the growing risks of state control of foreign borrowing. At the same time the state failed to play its expected role in the domestic economies: it changed from being a corrective mechanism to being a source of imbalances. Thus, *the way out of the crisis requires reconstruction of a financial market for the debtor coun-*

tries and a broader reassessment of the state's role in the economy.

Correction of disequilibrium ceases to be a theoretical exercise and becomes a precondition for the restoration of self-sustained growth. External illiquidity and internal inflation hold it back, and local economies become dangerously dependent on the erractic behavior of world markets.

The futility of econometric exercises designed to justify the current format of the external adjustment process resides in the extreme sensitivity of results — favorable or unfavorable — to the fluctuation of a handful of parameters: the growth of industrialized countries, external interest rates, and oil prices. Variation in these factors reflects the expected behavior of the world economy. *A longer-term adjustment strategy must take the exogenous factors into account and include mechanisms to absorb their impact on the domestic economy.*

I have tried to show that there are significant points in common to any strategy that will optimize the adjustment process. The unfeasibility of expecting the present disequilibrium to correct itself automatically is perhaps the most relevant: externally, paralysis of the financial market has killed hope for the replenishment of liquidity through the natural working of market forces; internally, there are no natural mechanisms for self-restraint in expansion of the public sector.

Concerted action will be needed both externally and internally to effect the degree of institutional change required. An orderly and consistent set of reforms is essential for triggering a favorable shock in expectations and truly bring about both a slowdown of inflation and the resumption of growth.

What is sought is a change in the terms of debt rescheduling that defines the supply of long-term resources and the equilibrium interest rate so that they will be attuned to external adjustment and growth.[1] The two are interconnected: a negotiated reduction of interest rates may be expected implicitly to generate a stable flow of new money over a pre-set period of time. It goes much further than mere multiyear refinancing of amortization.

The current practice, based on compulsory generation of megasurpluses in trade accounts, results in a net transfer of resources abroad on a nearly permanent basis. With the suggested alternative, *a more flexible negotiated external interest rate* is in essence an anticipation of events that should occur spontaneously. Prevailing market rates reflect a situation of momentary disequilibrium, a shift away from the long-term trend. To wait for deviations to be corrected naturally means prolonging unnecessarily the exposure of debtor countries to factors out of their control, and thereby generating a climate of uncertainty adverse to the recovery of private investment.

A number of technical alternatives exist to strike a suitable balance between a more flexible basic interest rate and stability of the international finance system. What is lacking is a political decision to move in that direction. The specific mechanism suggested here is quite simple operationally: *automatic capitalization of differentials observed between the market rate and a long-term shadow rate to be applied to rescheduling.*[2] In addition to establishing a protective net around the external accounts of debtor countries to shelter them from unpredictable interest rate fluctuations, this new approach would eliminate the need for countries to seek new money through the always inefficient path of compulsory syndication. Besides the positive effects associated with reducing the level of uncertainty, the new strategy would shift to debtor nations some decisionmaking power over the outcome of rescheduling, at present excessively concentrated in the creditors' hands.

Finally, by reducing the current profitability of financial assets, *interest rate flexibility is indirectly a powerful stimulus for the voluntary transformation of debt into capital.* It encourages a natural transition to a stage of debt stock restructuring side-by-side with the conventional refinancing of the flow of funds. It speeds the move out of the Age of Debt into a more promising and efficient Age of Capital.

Internally, new breathing room would contribute to a decompression of the real interest rate and a relief of inflationary pressures, thereby generating objective conditions for a gradual recovery of investment levels. External adjustment no longer would be a skewed process relying only on the trade balance account. Correction of external disequilibria would be achieved through direct action on the service and capital accounts, by the reduction of interest expenses and the gradual recovery of investment in risk capital. Trade surpluses would result from the relative efficiency of the domestic economy in its interaction with the outside world instead of from a forcibly produced residual designed to match rigidly pre-set conditions for external liquidity. It would follow that the exchange policy, without losing sight of its primary objective — to ensure real returns to the export sector — could be implemented with fewer inflationary side effects. This could be achieved in a market context through floating rates without the need to impose compulsory discretionary rules such as mini devaluations.[3]

New terms for external interest rates would reverse the current strategy for control of the public deficit. Now it is overly reliant on deep and real cuts in investment. Current spending could be decreased effectively by action on one of its major components, the debt service.

One virtue of the proposed solution is that it automatically becomes redundant when behavior of the world economy brings about a convergence between current and equilibrium interest rates. One can imagine a scenario so favorable to debtor country exports that they will no longer need to resort to new money. Such a possibility supports the priority of long-term restructuring, albeit as a simple contingency scheme in the event that reality moves away from good intentions and hopes. Nevertheless, should things develop according to the more favorable forecasts, the system will abolish itself automatically.

The rescheduling horizon must be changed simultaneously with comprehensive internal institutional reforms. Episodic monetary or credit policies cannot restrain public deficits over the long term. It is necessary to strike at the main sources of imbalance, the factors that generate permanent pressures to finance public deficits through borrowing and currency issues. It is essential to identify the scope and nature of this real disequilibrium and to place clear evidence before society that we cannot afford to live with it much longer. Governments must lead the way in the elimination of such imbalances, particularly in deciding the relative weight of spending cuts and tax increases. One thing is certain: regressive financing of public deficits by inflationary taxation is no longer tolerable.

Broad reforms of external and internal institutions and practices are vital if the adjustment process is to result in the recovery of investment levels, especially in the private sector. *Logical connections should be established between short- and long-term policies, between temporary adaptation and structural changes, between adjustment and growth.* Then we would move from a monetary crunch and fiscal expansion to fiscal restraint and monetary flexibility. Internal adjustment would lead to increased liquidity, in real terms a key element in reconciling the slowdown of inflation with the resumption of growth. In other words, internal adjustment would be achieved in the framework of declining real interest rates.

Expectations within the country should be improved by introducing tax and legislative reforms that will restore control of the state to society. Indexation should be reviewed only after these reforms have altered inflationary expectations. Once there is a break between the past and the future, redirection of the monetary correction system will follow. This sequence of actions will help extend the time frame of expectations by working as true insurance against inflation instead of stifling the economic system.

With expectations changed and inflation declining, compulsory monetary correction makes sense only for long-term contracts, as a safety device to guard against future uncertainties. The continuous slowdown of inflation gradually renders even this more limited role redundant, as both the labor and the financial markets are increasingly guided by expected inflation.

There are two key ideas behind my analysis. The first is that the *structural dimension* of the present crisis cannot be overcome by transitory intervention. It demands coordinated action and profound reforms. The second is the *concept of adjustment*. From the viewpoint of both fairness and efficiency, it is essential that adjustment extend to the international financial system and the industrialized nations. Unilateral adjustment by developing countries is politically unfeasible and economically inefficient. We have already seen that slight external ripples are sufficient to upset the fragile schemes for debt payments. This means that international banks cannot weather the storm unscathed; losses will have to be borne. The recent action of Japanese banks, followed by major American banks, in realizing losses and sharply increasing reserves is an important step. If necessary, developed countries will be forced to mobilize the necessary resources to prevent these losses from affecting their financial stability. The survival of the world economy is at stake.

Industrialized countries must not create additional obstacles to the already difficult process of growth resumption in developing countries either through their domestic policies or external actions, e.g., the U.S. policy on interest rates, protectionist trade policies, and the excessively conservative posture toward multilateral agencies. The multilateral institutions must adapt to new times: the voluntary withdrawal of private banks now demands their more active participation in financing the developing countries.

Orchestrated action is required. It must include a change in the policies of industrialized countries, innovation by the multilateral institutions (chiefly the IMF), new mechanisms to deal with short-term liquidity problems and long-term restructuring, and finally a new agreement between debtors and lenders. Such an agreement requires reformulation of the current policies of commercial banks. It entails the complexity of rehearsing an opera; but operas do get rehearsed. The alternative is chaos. Unilateral actions by developing countries may follow from any new exogenous event that renews uncertainties. Unilateral action becomes increasingly attractive so long as the current process of adjustment with recession or modest growth persists, and particularly if prospects for new bank credit become limited in the face of heavy interest payments.

Latin American countries realize the need for concerted political action around shared concerns. Together they demand that interest rates be included in the renegotiation rounds. After all, the international banks also try to reach a common strategy in advisory committees. Joint action by the LDCs can be expected to increase, particularly when interest rates or other external conditions turn unfavorable. Their joint action is a sword of Damocles over the future of the world economy, even after considerable strengthening of the capital base of major banks.

Another important objective is to adapt the IMF's role to the new and changing characteristics of the world economy. Despite its innovative role, the IMF does not wield sufficient political power and support to change the decisionmaking process for long-term external resources. Correction of external disequilibrium has been accomplished at the expense of a severe depression of international trade, with both recessionary and inflationary impacts on the domestic sphere.

With reference to internal adjustment, rigid methods and inflexible conditionalities assign a disproportionate weight to short-term issues, in spite of the IMF's own diagnosis that the problem is structural. The result is an accumulation of contradictions between program targets and results: after two years the Brazilian stabilization program ended up with a larger public deficit and higher inflation; the public asks whether the adjustment program was consistent even in its shorter-term objectives. Investments were penalized, particularly those of the private sector. In an excess of zeal, the connection between adjustment and development has been lost.

Yet the IMF is vital to the process. It must be reformulated and its resources reinforced. The rigidity of the present system of conditionalities is also a form of rationing the limited resources available to the IMF. Since the external debt rescheduling process and the adjustment efforts of debtor countries are expected to continue for a long time, the IMF's future role must be defined.

It would be unacceptable to have new guidelines for the IMF as a mere by-product of the renegotiations with private banks. The IMF is too important an institution to be reduced to the role of privileged auditor of international banks. Nor is it possible to fit the new idea of a multiyear IMF into the principle of equitable treatment of all member countries, as defined in its charter of principles.

It is precisely the need to find a new format for the love-hate triangle among the IMF, banks, and debtor countries that affords us the historic opportunity to review the IMF's practices in the framework of a new world economy. A new forum is needed in which fundamental discussion of these matters can take place. So far the debate has been disorderly and dispersed.

An enlarged Club of Paris might deal not only with government debts but also with the basic guidelines for renegotiation between banks and countries. It might be the international forum where consensus can be reached on long-term solutions to the problem of external indebtedness. The organization has the informal quality and the institutional flexibility essential for dealing with a problem requiring creativity and a dash of courage. Government authorities and representatives of multilateral organizations already meet under the Club of Paris to discuss rescheduling of government debts; all that is needed is to include the representatives of private banks' advisory committees. It would be a logical step, as everyone concerned, especially the private banks, now realizes that the sheer volume of loans made to debtor countries demands joint action by banks, governments, and multilateral organizations. For debtor countries, the entry of such new and distinguished guests would mean more than just setting additional places around the negotiation table. Under the new rescheduling framework, the relative bargaining power of debtor countries would increase substantially. It would then be possible to contrast the necessarily limited outlook of the banks, which focuses purely on the financial aspects, with the new economic, social, and geopolitical approaches certain to be brought into the discussion by government leaders.

On the internal side, the recommended institutional modernization would orient the notion of economic planning more toward a permanent evaluation of the public sector, in contrast to its posture in the recent past, which has been concerned basically with trying to offset market failures. The very real possibility of substantial allocative gains will foster the resumption of self-sustained growth with less severe disequilibrium. Expansion of the private sector will follow redefinition of the state's role and will be a major by-product of the institutional reforms. We also expect efficiency gains within the public sector, especially through greater decentralization of its actions. Finally, there will be improvements in productivity. Benefits already are accruing to the private sector from a reassessment of the industrialization-at-any-cost idea that has prevailed for years in Latin America. That view has generated profound structural changes, some of them at high social costs — glaring income inequities, explosive urbanization, and pockets of absolute poverty. Objective factors, such as the elimination of general subsidies and the correction of relative price distortions, are causing a healthy rediscovery of inherited comparative advantages, which is being reflected in a gradual transfer of resources from overly protected industries to more competitive areas, particularly to agriculture and mining.

In Brazil, the energy sector has undergone a significant structural change, both in the consumption profile now definitely adapted to the new cost matrix and in the replacement of imported oil by alcohol and other domestic substitutes such as electrical energy and domestic petroleum. This change has contributed to a sustainable improvement in the trade account. It is, however, the result of conscious investment requiring a long time to mature; it would not have happened through just a temporary restraint on demand.

The greater access to foreign markets achieved by the export drive increases domestic competitiveness within Brazil and allows continuous gains in efficiency. In a sense, exports provide for the correction of some distortions inherited from import substitution. In fact, there are examples of newly born industries that have grown in the shade of strong protectionist schemes and become strong exporters, internalizing productivity gains. Such is the case with the steel, paper, and automotive industries.

It is difficult to measure the precise impact of these allocative shifts. But the fact is that they will help the economy to achieve higher growth with the same overall savings through a significant rise in productivity. There is a convergence between allocative efficiency and distributive gains: the new dynamic sectors are generally labor intensive and inevitably lead to a relief of urban overcrowding.

Whether this economic and social potential is fulfilled will depend on institutional modernization by individual countries, particularly on the new pattern of public investment that emerges following fiscal discipline. If these new investments, especially in infrastructure and research, are directed to facilitate those allocative changes already under way in response to market signs, as well as to allow permanent gains in productivity, a new path of self-sustained growth can be achieved with a greater absorption of labor. That will make it possible to find a new development path with a high degree of social mobility. However, if we insist on the artificial development of new sectors of dubious economic profitability, the result will be a continuing pattern of cyclical and limited growth inevitably leading to more severe social unrest.

Recent events suggest a combination of factors leading to a new and more prominent stage in the debt crisis. Private banks, particularly the Japanese and American ones, have accelerated the process of raising reserves for nonperforming assets in developing countries and have explicitly realized losses, discontinuing some of their accounting gimmicks. The expected natural financial market recovery that should follow conventional rescheduling did not happen at all. It also suggests that the "Baker plan," which was approved at the Korean IMF meeting of 1985 and relied heavily on compulsory new money from private banks, is basically at an end after just a few experiments: Mexico (1986), Argentina (1987), and Philippines (1987).[4] Private banks now have less incentive to provide new money just to keep up the flow of interest payments.

With no signs that voluntary access to the financial market will reopen, and with a sharp decline in expected compulsory new money, the attractiveness of unilateral payment suspension by debtor countries will increase. In order to avoid the disruptive consequences for trade and investment of a prolonged stalemate in debt negotiations, it is essential that new ideas such as those discussed here — be put forth by leading creditor countries, particularly the United States.

With a reinforced capital base, even the U.S. banks can now examine realistic innovative proposals, such as partial interest capitalization. As a matter of fact, more radical transformations of debt into equity are being announced and quickly spreading among debtor countries. They are a new and promising market alternative that can throw light into the shadows of present bureaucratic debt negotiations.

Debt/equity swaps have many interesting economic features. The stock of debt is immediately reduced, and dividends replace the flow of interest payments. Of course, the newly generated capital may also be repatriated in the future. We should expect that minimum repatriation periods will be imposed to coincide with the maturity profile of rescheduled debt. There are, however, fundamental differences: dividends will be due only to the extent that the investment generates profits. The higher the domestic rate of return, the greater the incentive for reinvesting profits, and therefore the smaller the fraction of initial capital to be remitted. No such automatic compensating element exists in a pure indebtedness strategy. Concern is sometimes raised about the monetary impact of debt conversion. Of course, this measure makes sense only when inserted into a broader framework of adjustment with growth. Ideally it should be implemented at the same time as public deficit is being reduced. Swaps may therefore coexist with monetary control and decreasing inflation. Debt conversion could become a practical instrument to speed the reallocation of resources from the public to the private sector.

Finally, there are controversies over the role of the secondary debt market. The discount on country paper is a natural market development that cannot be hindered. It is a proxy, albeit imperfect, for future country performance, especially with respect to foreign exchange availability. It therefore should be appropriated by potential investors, reducing the cost of funds and offsetting unusually large risks. This discount may not necessarily affect at the margin the decision to invest. But it certainly has a powerful impact on the *timing* of the decision, which is exactly what is needed to maintain the level of private investment during the transition from debt refinancing to restructuring.

We cannot realistically expect that debt conversion alone will solve the present crisis. A larger role for government funds in the process appears inevitable given the instability of the world economy. Depending on the relative odds of two scenarios for the dollar the continuity of "soft lending" or reversion to a "free fall" in the years ahead, we may see a new wave of rising external interest rates that could strike a fatal blow to the great majority of debtor countries' economies. It is essential to anticipate this possibility and to begin to implement new schemes that will minimize the effects of unexpected external shocks.

On the domestic side, the frustrating Brazilian experience of 1986, when our country became a laboratory for "heterodox" economic experiments, practically demonstrated some of the basic issues raised in this book. First and most important is the need for a *simultaneous* process of coherent *internal* adjustment and deep change in *debt negotiation* terms and procedures.

Brazil has not followed either of these basic guidelines. The Cruzado plan made the mistake of trying to fight inflation just by freezing prices and wages. Disindexation was applied *prior* to correcting the basic sources of imbalance, particularly the public sector deficit. Therefore, the unilateral suspension of interest payments in February 1987 came, not as a planned step to inaugurate a more realistic round of negotiations, but as a desperate move to deal with the rapid depletion of our international reserves caused by the artificial expansion of domestic demand.

Under these circumstances, the Brazilian moratorium could not prevent sharp deceleration of the economy. Neither was it enough to restore adequate levels of external liquidity. On the contrary, it has enhanced uncertainties, squeezed export finance, and made the whole economic scenario worse.

The important lesson is that in economic policy the order of factors does alter the product. *People's expectations with respect to future inflation in Brazil will change only if a coherent set of institutional reforms geared toward the effective control of public sector imbalances is announced and implemented.* With the credibility of a consistent internal program established, it will be possible to transform the current pattern of debt refinance into a new stage of debt restructuring. The key, again, is symmetry between internal and external reforms.

Hope lies beyond the debt crisis. Through political action, present difficulties can be turned into future assets that will bring about a more balanced and self-sustained pattern of growth. It is essential to understand that this will not be a spontaneous occurrence. Actions oriented toward reforming the external and internal frameworks are vital. A change in mentality is also required, particularly the abandonment of myths that for so long have provided the basis for the development strategy of many countries, particularly in Latin America. Among these myths is the idea, at once naive and attractive, of unlimited growth through inflation. Another is the view that the state has special powers for bypassing constraints that in reality cannot be avoided. It would be a sad step backward to respond now with increased bureaucracy and less economic freedom.

The crisis and the dramatic events that have followed must prompt us to exorcise these ghosts once and for all and to construct our new development strategy on a sound and long-lasting foundation. To succeed, its driving energy must be the creativity and initiative of free individuals. That is our challenge.

Notes

Chapter 1

1. Resolution 63, adopted August 21, 1967, allowed banks to take external funds and lend them internally in cruzeiros at a cost equal to the exchange adjustment plus external interest rate and whatever margin the banks set. Subsequently, memos FIRCE 10 (September 12, 1969) and 20 (September 1, 1972), based on Law no. 4131 of September 3, 1962, authorized direct foreign borrowing by public and private institutions.

2. The United Nations Monetary and Financial Conference, called by the United States, started on July 1, 1944, in Bretton Woods, New Hampshire, and in just three weeks of discussions resulted in the establishment of the International Monetary Fund and the International Bank for Reconstruction and Development (IBRD), better known as the World Bank. The conference brought together 44 allied governments, including Brazil.

3. Nominal interest rates reached 20 percent in early 1980. Average annual figures moved between 12 percent and 16.6 percent from 1979 to 1982; this represents a real rate between 4 percent and 7 percent. (See Table 1.3.) If external interest rates are deflated by the export prices of each debtor country, the level of real rates is still greater.

4. Cline has estimated that, out of the external debt increase of non-oil-producing LDCs, assessed at $482 billion between 1973 and 1982, 83 percent might be attributed to exogenous shocks. The oil price hike in excess of world inflation would account for $260 billion; the jump in

real interest rates, $41 billion; terms of trade losses, $79 billion; and the drop in exports caused by world recession in 1981/82, another $21 billion. See William R. Cline, *International Debt and the Stability of the World Economy,* Institute for International Economics, Washington, D.C., September 1983.

5. In 1981 a major effort was made to curtail expansion of domestic credit, and interest rates under control since 1979 were deregulated. The result was a trade balance surplus and a slight slowdown of the inflationary process.

6. The figure given is the number of countries that had a formal agreement with the IMF before December 1984. A handful of other countries defaulted or rescheduled part of their debts before reaching an agreement with the IMF.

7. The U.S. Treasury Department has a contingency fund of unknown proportions, to be used at the discretion of the Chief Executive with no need for congressional authorization. The treasury can make very short-term loans with a maximum one-year maturity. The BIS began operating in May 1930 as an institution in charge of war settlements. It later developed into a sort of central bankers' banker, with whom industrialized countries deposit part of their international reserves. Neither institution, obviously, was able to deal with the acute liquidity squeeze following the Mexican default. For this very reason, in late 1983 the so-called General Agreement to Borrow was expanded and revamped. This emergency fund is fed by the top ten industrialized powers and can be set in motion, it is to be hoped, more effectively should the need arise again.

8. Since those loans have an average six-month maturity, $13 billion is just an estimate made on a *pro rata tempore* basis on loans maturing between September and December.

9. Dragoslav Avramovic, "Debts: Salient Features," in Khadija Hag (editor), *The Lingering Debt Crisis*, North-South Roundtable, Islamabad, Pakistan, 1985.

10. The Chilean mistake was in sticking with a fixed exchange rate despite the profound changes in external conditions, particularly the 1982 world recession, which had direct implications for the country's major single export, copper. Argentina likewise, in the same period, tried to use exchange policy as a tool against inflation in the presence of a growing public deficit fired by increased military spending.

11. Several studies have attempted to simulate the behavior of debtor countries as a function of the development of the world economy. Results vary enormously according to the basic assumptions adopted. See, for instance, William R. Cline, *International Debt*; and Rimmer de Vries,

The Debt Crisis: Problems and Prospects as Seen from the United States,
The Atlantic Conference, November 8–11, 1984.

12. The U.S. public deficit share of GDP was 5.8 percent in 1983.

Chapter 2

1. On the government side were the Minister of Finance, Ernane Galveas; the Minister of Planning of the Office of the President, Professor Antonio Delfim Netto; and I, as the President of the Central Bank of Brazil. A special tone was set at the meetings by the presence of Dr. Jacques de Laroisiere, Executive Director of the IMF.

2. Venezuela and then Colombia have rescheduled without a formal IMF program. Brazil has refinanced amortization payments and short-term loans without the presence of the Fund.

3. Those short-term standby agreements allow the country to resort to the so-called upper credit tranche, the portion of a country's quota in the IMF above the reserve tranche and the first credit tranche, access to which is almost automatic. The standby agreement is the formal acknowledgment of a stabilization program and therefore introduces the famous "conditionalities."

4. Under normal market conditions, loans of a certain magnitude are extended by pools of banks to allow a better distribution of risks. Thus the expression "syndicated loans," often used to describe what is commonly known as "jumbo loans." The term "quasi syndication" is used here as an attempt to distinguish between the conventional type of loan where the voluntary participation of banks is assumed, and the current system, where the share of each institution is compulsorily determined on a *pro rata* basis given its past commitments to the country.

5. The extended fund facility was set up in 1974 to cover longer-term adjustment programs than the conventional standby. Maximum duration of the program is three years, and loans mature at ten years, in comparison to the three-year maturity of standby programs. "New money" is a term that defines net loans (i.e., deducting amortizations) which means banks may extend loans just to refinance or rollover the principal. Any funds over and above such amounts are qualified as new money because they are in fact additional credits which may be used for new investments.

6. These margins are known as flat fees and commitment fees. In the rescheduling package of 1986 these fees were eliminated and spreads reduced (Table 2.2). LIBOR (Labor Interbank Offering Rate) is the base interest rate used as a reference for international loans. The prime rate

is used for preferred customers, supposedly the best and lowest-risk companies, in loan operations in the American financial market. Historically the prime rate has remained a few percentage points above the LIBOR, but over time the trend of both rates is quite similar.

7. In the United States, a special committee made up of officers from the Federal Reserve, Treasury, and the Controller of the Currency, among others, was set up to review periodically the credit standing of different countries. Their evaluation is based on objective elements (performance of IMF programs, regularity on interest payments), as well as subjective ones such as a commitment to eliminate arrears. Despite some flexibility by authorities in the application of these rules, appraisal of the market in terms of the bank's stock quotation is ruthless. This is an additional reason why banks are so anxious whenever interest payments are stopped.

8. Whenever the Central Bank of Brazil was formally sought by a financial institution, it would decide whether to authorize the start of negotiations abroad. The final word, however, came from the local monetary authority.

9. Rediscount needs of Brazilian banks ranged between US$400 and US$600 million per day. For the Continental Illinois rescue operation, approximately US$8 billion worth of special liquidity lines were involved.

10. *The Amex Bank Review, International Debt: Banks and the LDCs*, special paper no. 10, March 1984, London.

11. For the prospective analysis see, for example, the articles by Cline and de Vries. In the Brazilian case, de Vries estimates that the ratio of debt to exports will only be brought down to 200 percent, a magic number: once this level is reached, voluntary access of the country to the financial market would be resumed. Let us wait and see. . . .

12. Following the Brazilian moratorium, Citicorp, in May 1987, raised loan-loss reserves by $3 billion, initiating a new posture among American banks. German and Swiss banks have continuously reinforced their reserves and increased their capital basis since the outcome of the debt crisis. The Japanese banks have chosen a somewhat different strategy. In the beginning of 1987 they established a factoring company on Cayman island to allow a gradual transfer of certain sovereign debt. The company will buy the debt from the banks at a discount. Initial operations are related to 1983 Mexican loans but may be extended on a case-by-case basis to other countries. Funds to offset the discounted loans will be provided by the banks which will receive as a counterpart large tax breaks.

13. Absorption of external savings is normally measured by the current account deficit. It therefore represents the net inflow of real resources

from abroad. From this angle, for a set of countries, the trend is only one of strong reduction rather than necessarily being a net outflow of real resources. Mexico in 1983–1984 began to show significant surpluses in the current account side-by-side with the net outflow of financial resources. Both factors have been a major constraint on its potential growth. In the 1983–1986 period, Brazil has shown current account deficits and a substantial transfer of financial resources abroad.

14. A suggestion along the same lines was presented in an article I wrote for the journal *Euromoney*, published in September 1983, in which I put forth the idea of creating an "interest facility." See Carlos Geraldo Langoni, "The Way Out of the Country Debt Crisis," *Euromoney*, September 1983; see also my "Sharing the LDC Adjustment Burden," *Institutional Investor*, April 1984.

15. In strictly economic terms, the discounted value of expected returns on financial assets should not change significantly under the new system. The capitalization scheme assumes that in the future countries will be paying interest rates above current rates when the latter are below the long-term level of equilibrium. Such a period will be longer or shorter depending on the degree to which current market rates and shadow rates converge. Under the new arrangement, the degree of uncertainty is shifted from debtor countries to the financial system. Perhaps, under the circumstances, the financial institutions will promptly seek to ensure a higher income flow, which would justify the voluntary change from debt into capital.

16. There are many ways to achieve that goal. One is to extend the existing mutual fund mechanism to investments in the stock market (Law Decree No. 1401). The latter instrument would have the advantage of considerably expanding the basis of the stock market, making it possible for other corporations to become capitalized without any risk of waiving majority stock control.

17. There are additional suggestions for solving the external debt problem. In this book the emphasis is on principles rather than on specific guidelines. A very popular approach is to set a ceiling on interest payments as a ratio of exports. But this approach would bring severe uncertainty to banks regarding their returns, making it difficult for them to cope with the definition of nonperforming loans utilized by foreign regulators and auditors. Note that the concept of a long-term shadow interest rate, in addition to resting on a sound theoretical basis, assures a minimum amount of interest payments over time. For a very good summary of the different approaches, see *The Amex Bank Review*, Vol. II, No. 5, June 1984.

18. Erik Hoffmeyer, "The Real Solution to the Debt Crisis," paper presented at *Financial Times*, Tenth World Banking Conference, London, Decem-

ber 1984. Dr. Hoffmeyer gives an example: if marginal income tax equals 50 percent, inflation 5 percent, and nominal interest rates 10 percent, then the real interest rate before taxes is 5 percent, and zero after taxes. The problem is that, unlike an individual, a debtor country cannot deduct interest payments for income tax purposes. Therefore, net debtor LDCs pay a substantially higher real interest rate than domestic debtors in wealthy countries. Hoffmeyer's conclusion is that debtor countries are in theory entitled to a tax rebate that would be equivalent to a significant reduction in the interest rate in real terms. This would be the rationale to justify the use of resources from industrialized countries to set up an interest facility. The new tax law in the United States has changed this picture somewhat.

19. The multiyear Mexican rescheduling established an automatic refinancing of amortizations maturing through 1990, for 14 years with only a one-year grace period. The average spread throughout the period is 1 1/8 over LIBOR, in contrast to the previous 2 percent spread. Flat fees were eliminated. There are three controversial points, however. Mexico was supposed to pay about $1 billion of the debt principal in 1985. In other words, the grace period on the rescheduled amortizations had been reduced to a minimum. At the same time, the banks were allowed to finance part of their credit in local currency, which shifts the risk of any change in relative dollar exchange rates to the debtor country. There is also Clause 4, which defines a new role for the IMF, as explained in the text.

20. In 1984 nearly 30 percent of Brazilian exports were bought by the United States.

Chapter 3

1. Special Drawing Rights (SDRs) are a sort of international currency, which in the Fund serves as a means of payment in official transactions; the SDR is based on the weighted average of five key currencies (the dollar, the pound, the deutschmark, the franc, and the yen). It was created at the Rio de Janeiro IMF meeting in 1969.

2. Gross international reserves by the IMF definition are estimated at $11 billion at year-end 1984.

3. Until 1984, Venezuela was the single case where rescheduling took place without the IMF. Its favorable bargaining power at the time could be explained by its high level of international reserves (about $20 billion in 1982), and by the relatively low magnitude of its internal disequilibria (14 percent inflation in 1984). Columbia in 1985 and Brazil in 1986 followed a similar pattern, although in the case of Brazil there were no new credits involved.

4. The agreement provides for evaluation of the Mexican economic policy by the IMF twice a year, even after the current formal extention of the Fund agreement ends. This is a precondition for multiyear rescheduling.

5. See for example Robert A. Mundell's classic article "The Appropriate Use of Monetary and Fiscal Policy for International and External Stability," in Richard S. Thorn, *Monetary Theory and Policy*, New York, Random House, 1966. Also, Mario Henrique Simonsen, "The Developing Country Debt Problem," mimeographed, Graduate School of Economics, Getulio Vargas Foundation, February 1984.

6. Difficulties were so evident that, in the beginning of 1985, negotiations with the Fund were suspended. Since then Brazil has not tried another formal program where there is strong political opposition. This may change, however, in the near future.

7. Whenever one of the so-called "performance criteria" is not met, contractual provisions require interruption of IMF disbursements. To resume access to those credits, a waiver must be approved by the Fund's board of directors. The request for such a waiver must be supported by a listing of the corrective measures that, in principle, would put the program back on course.

8. The December 1984 letter of intention set a 120 percent inflation target for 1985. The time sequence of Brazilian letters of intention is as follows: 1/6/83 amended on 2/24/83; 9/15/83; 11/14/83; 3/15/84; 8/28/84; 12/20/84. The frequency of letters is, by itself, evidence of the internal inconsistencies in the adjustment program.

9. To reduce uncertainty and therefore minimize risks, any corporation or bank may redeposit in the Central Bank idle dollar resources: Resolution no. 595, circular letter no. 230, Resolution no. 432, Resolution no. 479, and Resolution no. 351. The Central Bank then becomes responsible for the cost of those loans. Such funds may be deposited temporarily or permanently. In December 1984 they amounted to $11 billion.

10. The total sales of ORTNs was Cr $1 trillion, equal to approximately 135 million federal bonds. Already in January these securities were taken out of the market.

11. This amount is computed by hypothetically reestimating the IMF quota value in 1983, assuming a ratio between the Fund's capital and international trade volume identical to the prevailing figure in 1945 (16.2 percent).

Chapter 4

1. The idea of inflation as tax is extremely simple. The tax rate in this case will equal the rate of growth in prices. The tax base is the amount of

money held by the public in the economy. By reducing the purchasing power of a given amount of money, inflation works like any other tax: it decreases the cash available for acquisition of goods and services, and transfers income mostly to the government and in part to banks, since some of the cash deposits (conceptually money) is not renumerated. Under expectations of increasing inflation, the public tries to cut monetary holdings to a minimum, which in turn reduces the inflation tax base. At the extremes of this process, the rate of growth in prices is so high and currency flight so intense that the government can no longer transfer real resources from the economy.

2. For an updated view of public sector behavior in Latin America, see Balassa, Bueno, Kuczynski, and Simonsen, *Toward Renewed Economic Growth in Latin America*, Institute of International Economics, Washington, D.C., 1986, Chapter 4.

3. A significant exception is Peru, where an independent central bank has been operating since 1980. Unfortunately, this by itself has not been enough to prevent growing inflationary pressures due to the general disorganization of the economy.

4. A once-and-for-all price increase can occur even in a noninflationary context. Inflation is defined as a continuous and generalized price increase. However, when increase in the price of a single commodity (such as oil) carries enough weight in the formation of expectations, the distinction between the two effects becomes considerably more complex. See Carlos Geraldo Langoni, Chapter 2, *A Economia da Transformacao*, Jose Olympio, Rio de Janiero, 1985.

5. In the 1981–1983 period the growth of money supply was strongly controlled and remained reasonably stable at around 70–90 percent. From the second half of 1983 through 1986, a fast monetary acceleration took place in response to the difficulties of effectively controlling the public deficit. Money supply grew to yearly rates of 304 percent in 1986 (Table 4.5).

6. Monetary correction was used in Brazil for the first time in 1964 with the issue of indexed treasury bills (ORTNs), precisely for the purpose of attracting noninflationary resources to finance the public deficit. In subsequent years it was extended to the tax system, wages, and the exchange rate.

7. As indicated in chapter 2, the shadow rate can be estimated as the historical value prevailing in the financial market, say through 1960–1980: around 6 percent in nominal and 2 percent in real terms.

8. The interest facility is described in detail in Chapter 2.

9. Some important qualifications are in order: the effect would be complete only so far as the new money required to finance the current account deficit could be generated implicitly through the partial capitali-

zation of interest. This seems to be the case for the major Latin American debtors. Even given this assumption, it might be argued that the reduction is merely temporary, since the difference between the reference rate and the market rate will have to be covered later. According to the approach I am suggesting, that payment will only be made when market interest rates are below the long-term equilibrium rates. In other words, in practice we would be anticipating the future fall of interest rates in real terms. In the new reference interest rate to be charged on the renegotiated debts, we would have to include a spread to reflect refinancing costs. Of course, new resources over and above the amount of interest to be capitalized would have to be lent at current rates, and would not be subject to capitalization. Otherwise a return to overborrowing would be encouraged, which obviously does not make sense.

10. For an excellent review of the end of German, Austrian, Polish, and Hungarian hyperinflation, see Thomas J. Sargent, "The Ends of the Four Big Inflations," Working Paper No. 158, Minneapolis, Minn.: Federal Reserve Bank of Minneapolis and University of Minnesota, October 1980.

11. This is one of the most important issues now under discussion by the Congress in the process of writing a new constitution.

12. The existence of open-end accounts, i.e., accounts on which no *a priori* credit expansion ceiling can be established, distorts the concept of a monetary budget and makes the monetary policy unmanageable. These accounts also help explain the existence during many years of the so-called movement account, which is in fact an automatic zero-cost rediscount line between Banco do Brasil and the Central Bank. Banco do Brasil is the chief agent in the implementation of programs tied to open-end accounts. It would be impossible to meet the needs of these programs with the bank's own resources. Some classic examples of these programs are: minimum prices, the oil account, wheat and sugar subsidies, social security, argricultural loans, and exports. An effort has been made in the last few years to eliminate these accounts by reducing several modalities of subsidized credit. Many distortions persist, however, and in fact a new movement account has been created recently between the Central Bank and state banks. It seems clearly infeasible to consider freezing those automatic sources of monetary expansion without first phasing out the primary sources that have fed open-end accounts. Once the chronic deficit is slashed, a legal constraint must be enforced to prevent its revival later on. Note that this reform is quite distinct from a mere discretionary decision by the executive to draw a broad line between Banco do Brasil and Central Bank accounts or even to substitute the scheme with Treasury advances, as was done recently without practical results. A legal constraint on the deficit needs

to be approved by the national Congress.

13. Sales grew at an outstanding monthly rate of 15 percent. Stock prices went up by 112 percent between March and May. The differential between free market exchange rate and the official level reached 100 percent.

14. The government would still set the minimum wage and public service salaries with full *expost* offsetting of any gap between estimated and effective inflation after a sufficiently long period. Wage flexibility would further facilitate the reconciliation of inflation slowdown and economic reactivation.

15. Again, an excellent example was the change from the cruzeiro to the cruzado, which followed the general freeze on prices and wages in February 1986. With inflation running around 20 percent per month in the first months of 1987, it is difficult to recall any important gain from the monetary reform itself.

16. The production of EMBRAER Bandeirante aircraft and synthetic quartz are important examples of the economic possibilities of investment in basic and applied research in developing countries. Research on new crop varieties is another classic example of an area where indigenous research efforts are vital to the economy.

Chapter 5

1. U.S. Senator Bill Bradley (D-New Jersey) declared in a June 1986 speech, "Creditors should offer debt and interest rate relief in exchange for debtor reforms designed to restore balance to North-South trade, to revive hopes for widely shared economic progress, and to strengthen the international financial system." He called for "a partnership for growth between developing debtor nations and industrialized creditors." See his "Proposal for Third World Debt Management," Zurich, Switzerland, June 29, 1986.

2. Since I originally presented this idea in a 1983 article in *Euromoney*, many other alternatives have been suggested. For a good summary, see C. Fred Bergsten, William R. Cline, and John William, *Bank Lending to Developing Countries: The Policy Alternatives*, Institute of International Economics, Washington, D.C., 1985.

   Three are of particular interest. One suggestion is to substitute long-term inflation-indexed bonds for present debt to the banks, with the inflationary components capitalized and debtor countries paying a real rate of interest. The attraction of this idea lies in the possibility of placing this newly created bond with nonbanking institutions, such as pension funds, at the same time that the interest burden is reduced, at least on a cash flow basis. Another innovative proposition is the creation of an institution to buy, probably at market price, some of the Third World debt, the basic funding of which would be provided by the issuing of SDRs. The fact that such a revolutionary idea is even being considered by the United States Congress suggests how much the way of looking at the debt problem has changed over the past few years.

A third proposal, both thoughtful and comprehensive, is offered by Bill Bradley. Op. cit.

"[A] summit [conference] should include representatives of the governments of all major creditor countries, as well as small and large banks from Europe, the U.S., Canada and Japan. . . .

"As a goal and only a goal for the total value of yearly trade relief packages that the summit would offer to eligible countries, I suggest:

3 points of interest rate relief for one year on all outstanding commercial and bilateral loans to eligible countries;

3 percent write-down and forgiveness of principal on all outstanding commercial and bilateral loans to eligible countries; and

3 billion dollars of new multilateral project and structural adjustment loans for eligible countries.

"Trade-debt relief packages should be country-specific . . .[T]he value of each yearly trade relief package should depend on the uses that each debtor has made of a previous year's package. I propose six guidelines that suggest the goals behind trade relief packages while recognizing that debtor reforms must come from within. Debtors should:

1) liberalize trade so their industries and consumers can purchase competitively priced goods and services from the U.S. and other industrialized countries;

2) reverse capital flight since there is no reason for outsiders to invest in Third World countries if their elites will not invest in their own future;

3) encourage internal investment to promote self-reliance rather than dependency on external finance;

4) pursue domestic policies that promote economic growth;

5) choose policies that have broad internal political support; and

6) keep debt management free from scandal.

"A trade-debt relief summit that brings creditors together to consider coordinated debt relief has strong potential to rekindle growth in developing countries . . ."

3. The exchange risk involved in the expectation of new levels of real devaluation would be nearly eliminated. It is interesting to remember that between 1968 and 1979, Brazil consistently followed a pattern of exchange devaluation consistent with domestic inflation after deduction of world inflation.

4. The plan proposed by James Baker III, Treasury Secretary of the United States, mentioned a great effort by industrialized governments and multinational agencies, but the share of private banks in providing new finance was still disproportional. The plan also restated the model of adjustment with the IMF that has been tried since 1982.

Selected Bibliography

The Amex Bank Review, "International Debt: Banks and the LDCs," Special Papers 10, London, March 1984.

Avramovic, Dragoslav; "Debts," United Nations North-South Round Table, Vienna, September 1984.

Bela Balassa, Gerer M. Bueno, Pedro Pable Kuczynski, Mario Henrique Simonsen, *Toward Renewed Economic Growth in Latin America*, Institute for International Economics, Washington, D.C., 1986.

Calverley, John, "Restoring Creditworthiness," *The Amex Bank Review*, Special Papers 9, January 1984.

Cline, William R., *International Debt and the Stability of the World Economy*, Number 4, Institute for International Economics, Washington, D.C., September 1983.

De Vries, Rimer, "The Debt Crisis: Problems and Prospects as Seen from the United States," The Atlantic Conference, Foz do Iguacu, Brazil, November 1984.

Hoffmeyer, Erik, "The Real Solutions to the Debt Crisis," Paper presented at the *Financial Times* Tenth World Banking Conference, London, December 1984.

Kaletsky, Anatole, *The Costs of Default*, a Twentieth Century Fund Paper, Priority Press, New York, 1985.

Killick, Tony, ed., *The Quest for Economic Stabilization: The IMF and the Third World*, London, Heinemann Educational Books, 1984.

Kuczynski, Pedro Pable, "Latin American Debt," *Foreign Affairs*, 61, Winter 1982/83.

Langoni, Carlos Geraldo, *A Economia da transformacao*, Jose Olympio, Rio de Janiero, 1983.

_____, "The Way Out of the Country Debt Crisis," *Euromoney*, September 1983.

_____, "Sharing the LDC Adjustment Burden," *Institutional Investor*, April 1984.

_____, "Country Debt Problems: the Brazilian Case," *Cato Journal*, 4, Spring/Summer 1984.

McKanzie, George W., *The Economics of the Eurocurrency System*, New York, Macmillan, 1976.

Meigs, A. James, "Regulatory Aspects of the International Debt Problem," Seminar on the World Debt and the Monetary Order, Washington, D.C., January 20, 1984.

Mehran, Hassanali, ed., *External Debt Management*, Washington, D.C.: International Monetary Fund, 1985.

Mohammed, Azizali F., "Fund Conditionality: An Insider View," United Nations NorthSouth Round Table. Santiago, Chile, February 1984.

_____. "Recent Fund Role in External Debt Management," United Nations NorthSouth Round Table, Vienna, September 1984.

Nowzad, Bahram, "The Extent of IMF Involvement in Economic Policy Making," *The Amex Bank Review*, Special Papers 7, London, September 1983.

Sachs, Jeffrey D., "External Debt and Macroeconomic Performance in Latin America and East Asia," *Brookings Papers on Economic Activity* 2, 1985.

Sargent, Thomas J., "The Ends of Four Big Inflation". Working Paper 158, Federal Reserve Bank of Minneapolis and University of Minnesota, October 1980.

Simonsen, Mario Henrique, *The Developing Country Debt Problem*, Mimeographed, Graduate School of Economics, Getulio Vargas Foundation, Rio de Janiero, February 1984.

_____, *Developing Debtor Country Prospects and OECD's Macro Economic Policies*, Mimeographed, Graduate School of Economics, Getulio Vargas Foundation, Rio de Janiero, September 1984.

Index

About the Author

Carlos Geraldo Langoni was Brazil's principal representative at its 1982–83 debt negotiations. He was at the time 35 years old, the youngest ever president of his country's Central Bank. Currently he is professor at the Getulio Vargas Foundation Graduate School of Economics, São Paulo, and director of its center for World Economy.